"Is he all right?" I inquired. I cou[...]
ing.

"I don't think he's okay. Nobody says anything."

I decided to delve more deeply. "Let's find out what happened to him. I'm going to tap you on the forehead and count backwards from three to one and find out what happened to your older brother. Three, two, one. Now you can remember."

The tapping helps to deepen the hypnotic level even more, enhancing memory recall.

"He was shot," she suddenly recalled.

"He was shot?"

"I'm so sad!" She began to sob, her whole body convulsed by tragic emotion.

"I know. It's okay. Was it an accident?"

"I don't think so. I think it wasn't an accident." She was sobbing less now.

"No. And you miss him."

"My little brother can't remember him." The crying stopped as she observed this detail.

"It happened a while ago?"

"It happened when he was a baby."

"When your little brother was a baby. It's okay. But you were older; you remember. Let's go back before he was shot so that we can see him and find him. You can remember. It's okay. This was a long time ago. When I count to three, go back before he was shot so that you can remember him. Moving back in time . . . one, before he was shot . . . two, your older brother . . . three, before he was shot, now. You can remember."

"Oh, God, it's John. It's my brother John!" Andrea had found that her older brother in this past lifetime had returned in her current life as her brother John. She was still very sad, but now I could help heal her grief.

"Now you know, and it's okay because he came back as

John. You don't have to be sad anymore. You can see connections and see that he's okay. He's fine. But you missed him a lot *then* and it explains a lot about your relationship to your brother, John."

Actually I didn't know anything about Andrea's relationship to John. In view of her powerful emotional reaction to his death in their shared past life, however, I assumed lingering patterns and effects would have emerged in their current-life relationship.

"Were you ever afraid of losing him?"

"He was sick when he was a baby."

"What happened?"

"He was born premature."

"Before you?"

"After me."

"After you." Andrea looked as if she might start crying again. "Okay. It's okay now. A lot of things can come together for you now, about John, about life. What are you experiencing now? What do you remember?"

"I'm still sad."

I decided to progress her within that lifetime.

"Let's go ahead in that girl's life. Let's go ahead in her life. It's well after her brother has been shot; it's after that now. Let's go to another important event in her life. She's older now; it's after her brother."

Her face brightened almost immediately.

"Now I can shoot guns," she proudly proclaimed. Andrea's mood had completely changed.

"Now you can shoot guns?" I echoed.

"I'm really good. I'm good at target practice. I can outshoot all the boys. And I have different shoes."

"Now you have your own?"

"And all the boys are flirts, because they think it's cool that I can shoot a gun."

"You're not so isolated now?" I inquired.

"No. There're more houses. Not a lot, but there's a road, and there are people who come and go. I'm older. It's fun."

"These are happier memories now: the flirting, your skill with a gun." I wanted her to stay with this scene and its happier ambience.

"They're teasing me, but they admire me," she added.

"Can you see yourself, what you look like? You must have been very pretty, with all this flirting going on for you."

"Brown hair, and it's in curls just beyond my shoulders. I have a blue ribbon in my hair, and it's pale blue, and I have a skirt that has a pattern on it, like a little flower pattern. My shirt is white or pale pink. It's just a normal shirt; it's not that fancy. But I feel like my brother wasn't there so I learned to . . . wanted to . . . feel this pressure, this pressure to be like one of the boys."

"To kind of take his place?"

"I just want to be able to take care of myself," Andrea clarified.

"Yes, and you do a good job of that. You've learned how to shoot, to handle a gun, as well, if not better, than the boys. What about this flirting, though? Is there anyone that kind of—"

She cut me off.

"They're all just sort of yucky."

"Okay. Let's move ahead in time again now. I'll count to three. Move to the next important event in her life, the next important event. One, two, three. Be there. You're older now. What happens?"

"She has her own place. I'm watching her." Andrea was more the observer now, watching herself in that lifetime on the Great Plains.

"Good. You can watch her or you can go into her—whatever you're more comfortable with."

"She lives all by herself."

"She didn't marry?"

"Never found anybody. She always thought she was too good for any of those boys. She's not lonely. She's got sort of a ranch, and there are people who work for her. They like her. She's fair. . . ." Andrea's voice trailed off as she watched the scene. I began to progress her ahead in time.

"So she's very, very competent. She's made her own ranch. She has employees and is very capable. This was difficult for a woman of those times, too. She must be very strong. Let's go to the end of her life now, to the very last day, the last moments. If it is at all uncomfortable you can float above it, but if not, stay with it. On the count of three, let it all come in to focus, the very last day of that life. One, two, three. Be there. Go ahead to that and see what's happening and if anyone is around."

Andrea seemed very calm. "There's nothing exciting; she's just very peaceful. She's old. Nobody's left anymore.

"But she's okay," Andrea added. "She's had a really good life, and she's not sick. She looks okay; she's just old. She's got a white dress with a high neckline. She's just sitting there, just looking out, just sitting on the porch."

"Is that where she dies?"

"I think so."

"Just float above now, float above. Leave that old body. You'll feel so light and free as your spirit floats above. Perhaps you can look down and see her, her body there below. And then, feeling so free and so light, review that life, the lessons that she learned, that you learned. What did you learn? What did she learn?"

"She learned not to be afraid of being alone. She learned to take care of herself," Andrea answered from a higher perspective.

"Yes, to be independent," I observed.

"Very independent. She really *liked* her life. People made fun of her because she never got married and she never had children. She never seemed to care. The people in the community liked her. They stopped making fun of her later in life. People liked working for her. She had lots of cattle."

"In this floating state now, see if you become aware of what happens next. You've left the body; you're floating. What happens next? What do you become aware of?"

"I'm going up, and she's getting smaller. I'm just floating. I'm just in a blue light; I'm just floating."

"Good. Feeling okay, no more illness, not old, just floating. Your consciousness goes on. What happens next? Or do you just stay floating?"

"There are just rays of blue light, and they are coming above the left side of my head, but it's a big cone of blue light, and I can't see beyond the cone. . . ." Again, a long period of silence followed.

"Is there anything more?" I finally asked, wanting to know more about the cone of blue light.

"No. . . ."

"Okay. Are you ready to come back now?" Andrea nodded yes.

"Good. Make the connections before you come back between her life on the prairie and her independence and yours."

Television cameras or not, Andrea was learning some important lessons. She quietly processed her "new" data. Then she smiled broadly.

"I *really* like her."

"That's good. You have a lot of her strength, you've carried that over. This is very good. And also, you know that your brother is back. So death is not what it seems. People come back."

"I missed him so much." Another twinge of sadness crossed her face.

"I know," I answered. "But she still became very strong and independent. Relationships are very important, and independence is, too, when they're balanced. And he's back! And this time, even though it was a little precarious when he was an infant, he lived this time. So you could be reunited. That's how souls work and love works. We're always being reunited. So let go of any sadness or fears of loss that way. We always come back together, again and again. Remember also the love and the proud obnoxiousness of your father, the love of your mother coming into this life with you again, the recognition that was there. They were on the prairie, too. The happiness of the snow and your dog, your father and his parka. All of that love that you've carried through in this life, where you've managed to have relationships and independence and strength and love, and you've balanced it all. You've done all of these in a wonderful balance. That's wonderful. So feeling her strength and independence and your ability to make really good relationships, bring all of this positive thought and feeling back with you."

At this point, after digesting all of this information and experiencing so many emotions, Andrea looked tired. I decided to awaken her. She had learned enough for this day.

"In a few moments I'm going to awaken you by pressing upwards on your forehead at a point between your eyebrows. When I press upwards, you can open your eyes, and you will be awake. You'll be alert, and in full control of body and mind, feeling wonderful, feeling great, lighter, as if a load has been lifted off your shoulders, because the sadness from losing the brother of that time will be gone now. You know he's back. And feeling so peaceful, so relaxed and yet in full control. When I press upwards you can awaken completely." I pressed upwards on Andrea's forehead, and she slowly awakened.

"Take your time and come all the way back. You did fine. How do you feel?"

"Pooped."

"Pooped," I repeated, empathizing with her. I became aware that I was tired too; my concentration had remained strongly focused. "It's intense. A lot of work. Was it what you expected?"

"I didn't know what to expect. I never expected to see my brother. I thought I'd see maybe one of my daughters, but she wasn't there. I felt like I was being pulled to another time, a different life, but I couldn't get there, I just couldn't get there. I could see where it was but I couldn't get there."

"A third place?"

"Yeah, I couldn't get there."

"Do you know what that time was?"

"No. It was before that prairie lifetime, but I just couldn't get there. It was like there was this stream of blue light, but it was a pure cone and it just ended. Like the first one, where it was completely surrounding me, and I just suddenly saw feet. This one was . . . I could see the edge of the light and you could tell where it just stopped. It was dark on the outside. It was like someone had taken a cone and put it over me. It ended and it was like, right there."

Apparently Andrea could glimpse the other past life, perhaps a lifetime with her daughter, but she could not navigate past the brilliant blue light.

"It's just to let you know that it's there, but it wasn't for now. That's okay. It's there too, and you've had connections with your daughters, I'm sure, also. But you found your brother— not what you expected. That's one of the characteristics of this; you don't always get what you expect. That was a surprise. But apparently there was some sadness."

Andrea immediately concurred. "It was such a surprise because it's such a happy lifetime this time. My brother and I are very close, but of all the kids, he's the one who was sick right after he was born. But I didn't expect to see his face."

"And the intensity of the emotion is very powerful, because it's right there and it's so real. You could *feel* the sadness, you could *feel* the separation. But when you were seven or eight in this life you felt the positive emotion of walking with your father, which was a very—"

"It was a *great* memory," she interrupted.

"Yes, that's a great memory," I agreed. Andrea's eyes seemed to glaze over as she once again recalled the childhood scene.

"I could feel the wind on my face. I could remember the snowflakes. I could see it all. I could remember every bend, and those streetlights, I'd *forgotten* them," she marveled.

"I think we remember everything," I added, "so this is one way to remember that kind of detail, that feeling of snowflakes, the bend of the road, how your feet felt. All of these feelings. It's more than emotion—physical sensations too."

"So everything I talked about, I'll remember? And then more?"

"Sure, you remember more. For example, I let you linger awhile with the birth thing."

"I couldn't get out of her," Andrea remembered. "It was dark and it was a long tube and I couldn't get out of her."

"You were taking longer there; I thought you were out. That was the darkness you encountered. You just weren't born yet. But you remembered a man coming into the next bed to want to have sex with his wife who had just delivered a baby, and that was vivid to you, and yet you were just born yourself. That was interesting too, that that kind of detailed memory would come to you."

"My mother was not happy," Andrea repeated once again.

"I know."

"She turned me away. She turned me." Andrea was remembering even more details now. Even though awake now, she could still recall the hospital scene.

"She would probably have left the room if she were stronger," I added.

Andrea snapped back to the present time.

"Is there a norm for a first time?" Andrea asked, returning to her role as a reporter.

"Perhaps about fifty percent will have some sort of memory. But yours were so vivid and so intense for the first time that it would be like in the upper fifteen or twenty percent. Only about fifteen percent of the people can do that. And this technique would work for you at many different levels, not just memories," I added. "You can learn to control your body. For example, if we needed to lower your blood pressure, you could probably do it this way, without medicine. Fall asleep—like that," I said, snapping my fingers. "You could have gone like that. You can use it for physical reasons, for health reasons. If there were phobias, we could find a cause and get rid of them."

"There were some places I've traveled where I've always thought I've been before. The West is one of them; Russia . . . is another."

Even after the television cameras were turned off and the recording ceased Andrea remained in a calm state, musing about her experiences during the regression.

"He was killed by a long gun," she added. "By a rifle, not a pistol."

She was adding details. People undergoing regressions are aware of hundreds of details, many more than they supply during the questioning while they are immersed in the trance state, remembering the childhood and past-life experiences. She continued to reflect and remember.

"When John was born in this life, he was jaundiced. The nurses came to take him for treatments, and my mother said to them, 'I'll probably never see him again. He's probably going to die.'"

When her mother had handed her newborn son to the nurses, she began to detach somewhat from her baby, in a sense preparing for his death. Although she loved him very much, this guarding of her emotions existed even after John gained strength and his health dramatically improved. In a sense, her mother was always anticipating the death of this child.

In cases of newborn jaundice, which is fairly common, the liver chemical bilirubin is temporarily elevated, causing jaundice, or a yellowing of the skin. Putting the baby in natural light or under lamps of a certain light frequency is usually enough to break down the excess bilirubin and restore the skin to normal. As the liver matures, the jaundice is entirely cured. This whole healing process may take only a few days or a week or two.

Andrea's mother overreacted to her son's newborn jaundice. As the wife of a doctor, she must have realized that John's life was not in jeopardy. According to Andrea, John was always aware of his mother's reserve, although he had no understanding of why he was singled out this way.

"Do you see the connection?" I asked Andrea. "Your mother was also John's mother in that prairie lifetime last century. He was killed then. She lost him. When he came back as her infant son in this life and then developed jaundice, she remembered the previous loss. Perhaps she didn't remember consciously, but emotionally or subconsciously, she did remember. So she protected herself by keeping her emotions in check. She couldn't bear to lose him again. She really believed he was very fragile, like before, and that he would leave her again."

Andrea was ready to burst with excitement. Her regression had explained the relationship between her mother and her younger brother. She now knew the real roots of her mother's behavior and her brother's reaction to the protective barrier his mother had erected in case she lost him again. Andrea would explain everything to them.

From the many regressions I have facilitated and studied, Andrea's was a classical one, filled with healing memories, intense emotions, and vivid recollection of details. Moreover, she possessed a super-conscious ability to learn the lessons of her past lifetimes and to connect them to the lessons of her current life.

The television segment never aired. An executive at the network feared that because the piece was so vivid and so emotional, Andrea might compromise her credibility as an objective reporter.

Thus, millions of people were deprived of the chance to learn more about the nature of life, about how we are all connected and responsible for each other, about the horrors and devastation of killing, and how the effects of violence spill over into subsequent lifetimes.

After Andrea made the connection between her brother's past death and her mother's current-life fears, she grew silent. I could see that she was still contemplating, still experiencing the intense feelings the regression had triggered. I, too, grew silent. This was a private time for her, and I did not want to interview her further in front of her television colleagues. Often, these experiences can be both intense and transcendent—too personal to share—so I simply looked at her radiant face.

I was filled with great compassion for the individual beside me, and my heart was lifted. My own consciousness began to shift. The hot, crowded room faded away. The traffic noises, sirens, and constant background chatter of human voices ceased. I was no longer completely aware of my body. I became aware of a beautiful light in the periphery of my vision.

A voice whispered at the borders of my mind, at the extreme edge of my awareness. I believe it was a Master:

"When you look at another person, in relationship, in therapy, in life, see their soul through lifetimes and eons of time. Not just the transitory physical being across from you. You, too, are such a soul."

The voice spoke softly and lovingly and with deep compassion. This was advice, not criticism.

I gazed gently back at Andrea, seeing both her and the frontier girl. I knew she also had many other lifetimes, many other names. But her soul was always the same. I needed to see *that* part of people, which remains constant—their souls—not their transitory physical forms, to really understand and to help. To help them and also to help myself, for I too am such a soul.

You are as well.

Many of my patients who have recalled distant memories similar to Andrea's have experienced a dramatic diminishing or even the disappearance of their chronic symptoms.

For example, I regressed a fifty-year-old South American woman who suffered from profound claustrophobia, a fear of being trapped in small or enclosed places. She had been afflicted with this phobia since her early childhood. In the regression she remembered being entombed alive when she was an Egyptian slave whose owner, a relative of the pharaoh, had died. It was the custom for some slaves to be buried alive with the noble so that they could serve him in the afterlife. The slaves were given a poison to ingest before they suffocated in the small enclosed interior of the burial tomb. After this memory her claustrophobia disappeared and has never returned.

What is the mechanism of this clinical improvement?

I believe there are at least two explanations, although other factors are assuredly also at work. In my experience, the recall of repressed or forgotten traumatic, often painful memories is often associated with healing. Recalling these events with their associated emotions, called catharsis or abreaction in clinical terms, is a cornerstone of psychoanalysis and other traditional psychotherapies. The very act of bringing such buried memories into consciousness is extremely helpful. My findings indicate that the therapeutic arena needs to be enlarged, that we cannot stop the psychic archeology at childhood or even infancy, but that past-life patterns and memories also must be excavated for complete healing to occur.

The second reason that these memories promote clinical improvement is that as we experience ourselves in other bodies and in ancient times, as we watch our many deaths and rebirths, we are filled with the sure and unerring realization that we are eternal souls, not just individual bodies. We never really die; we merely change our levels of consciousness. Because our loved ones are immortal too, we are never really separated from them. This realization of our true spiritual nature is a powerful healing force.

Just as each facet of a diamond mirrors the whole, Andrea's regression experience reflects the major themes of this book.

She recalled memories and feelings from the fetal state, before she was actually born. She was also aware of her parents' emotions, demonstrating that consciousness is "non-local," not limited to our physical bodies or brains. This alone implies that when we die, our consciousness survives and goes on, since it is not physically based. Of course, memories of dying in past lives and of what happens after death also confirm the continuing existence of consciousness. Andrea, for example, was able to observe the old woman's body that she had just vacated.

Andrea was able to recall incidents that happened mere moments after her birth in this lifetime. Infants and young children are aware of so much more than we suspect. They are aware of our emotions as well as our actions. The flow of our loving feelings and thoughts to them, both before and after birth, nourishes their souls and is vital for healthy development.

Through memories recalled during her regression, Andrea learned how past-life and perinatal events can profoundly influence current-life connections. Andrea found her current parents and brother in her past-life memory. She learned that we are always reunited with our loved ones. Sometimes the reunion occurs on the other side, in other dimensions; sometimes the reunion takes place in a future lifetime together, back here on earth.

She was able to discern which values in life are important and which are unimportant or even damaging. She learned about the pain that guns and violence can cause. Every life is precious.

After she died in her lifetime on the Great Plains, Andrea found a cone of beautiful blue light. There are many other descriptions, both later in this book and in other sources, of people encountering a beautiful and replenishing light after leaving their bodies. This encounter occurs during NDEs, and apparently after death as well. A loved relative or friend or a spiritual being is often waiting at the light to greet the out-of-body traveler and to impart important information or messages.

Messages from the other side, as well as other forms of psychic or paranormal phenomena, will be examined in much more detail in a later chapter. We all possess intuitive abilities far beyond what we realize. As you integrate the stories, experiences, and exercises in this book, you will be able to hone your intuitive perceptions and receive information and messages more directly. Some of you will become healers for others.

The energy of love pervades and unifies Andrea's entire regression. Her parents' love, her love for her brother, the reunion with loved ones. Even the cone of blue light felt very warm, comforting, and loving, she later confided to me.

Andrea's experience of this energy in several of its manifestations will allow her to express her own love more openly and completely in her current life and relationships. She will also be more comfortable in accepting the love of others, because love flows both ways, encompassing both giving and receiving.

Ultimately, Andrea's profound regression experience will lead her to a greater understanding of the nature of her life and soul. Such an understanding is a sacred step. Such steps are accompanied by positive changes in the present life: better physical and emotional health, healthier relationships, more happiness and joy.

As you share the experiences of the people you will meet in this book, and ponder the messages of the Masters and consider my stories and reflections, I hope that you too will be walking these steps to wisdom.

Once you begin, you will approach the obstacles and frustrations in your life with more patience and calm. Through understanding your past lessons and debts, you will remember your goals for the current life. You will feel fulfilled and no longer confused or lost. You will learn to overcome fear, anxiety, and grief. You will live your life more fully in the present moment, and you will enjoy its pleasures more completely. Above all, you will understand what we all have in common:

We are beyond life and death, beyond space and beyond time. We are all immortal, and we exist throughout eternity.

❦ CHAPTER THREE ❦

Coming Back

We choose when we will come into our physical state and when we will leave. We know when we have accomplished what we were sent down here to accomplish. . . . When you have had the time to rest and re-energize your soul, you are allowed to choose your re-entry back into the physical state.

Not accidentally or coincidentally are we born into our families. We choose our circumstances and establish a plan for our lives before we are even conceived. Our planning is aided by the loving spiritual beings who eventually guide and protect us while we are in our physical bodies as our life's plan unfolds. Destiny is another name for the unfolding dramas we have already chosen.

There is considerable evidence that we actually see the major events in the life to come, the points of destiny, in the planning stage prior to our births. This is clinical evidence, gathered by myself and other therapists from our patients who have experienced pre-birth memories while under hypnosis, during meditation, or through spontaneous recall. Mapped out are the key people we will meet, our reunions with soul-mates and soul companions, even the actual places where these events will eventually occur. Some cases of déjà vu, that feeling of familiarity, as if we have been in that moment or that place before, can be explained as the dimly remembered life preview coming to its fruition in the actual physical lifetime.

The same is true for all people. Often, people who were adopted wonder whether their life plan has been somehow disrupted. The answer is no. Adoptive parents are chosen as well as the biological ones. There are reasons for everything, and no coincidences exist on the path of destiny.

Although every human being has a life plan, we also have free will, as do our parents and everyone with whom we interact. Our lives and theirs will be affected by the choices we make while in physical state, but the destiny points will still occur. We will meet the people we had planned to meet, and we will face the opportunities and obstacles that we had planned long before our births. How we handle these meetings, however, our reactions and subsequent decisions, are the expressions of our free will. Destiny and free will co-exist and interact all the time. They are complementary, not contradictory.

The consensus of evidence from my regression patients is that the soul appears to make a reservation for a particular physical body around the time of conception. No other soul can occupy that body. The union of body and soul is not completed, however, until the moment of birth. Before this time, the soul of the unborn child can be both in and out of the body, and it is often aware of experiences on the other side. It may also be aware of events outside its body and even outside the mother's body.

The soul can never be harmed. Neither miscarriages nor abortions harm the soul. When a pregnancy does not come to term, it is not unusual for the same soul to occupy the body of a subsequent child of the same parents.

After I gave a lecture on paranormal phenomena, a graduate psychology student told me about a dream he had had when his wife was four months' pregnant. At that time, the sex of the fetus was not known. One night, his unborn daughter came to him in a vivid dream, announcing her name, describing her immediate past life, and explaining why she was choosing to be born to this young couple, her karmic purpose and plans. He awoke with the riveting dream sharply etched in his mind. He turned toward his wife. "I just had the most amazing dream," he began, at which point she cut him off.

"Me too!" she exclaimed. "I dreamt our daughter came to me. . . ." Same name, same past life, same plans, same details, *same dream.*

They were both shocked. That both mother and father received the very same message during simultaneous dreams served to validate the information and to make the knowledge even more powerful.

Five months later, a beautiful baby girl was born to them.

Marie, an Italian woman in her late fifties, was amazed by the vividness (and what turned out to be the accuracy) of her recall for an incident a month before her birth, when she was yet in the womb.

Marie had never been hypnotized or regressed before, and she was having a difficult time accepting her experiences as actual memory, even though the detail and clarity were amazing to her.

"I kind of don't believe it," she began. "When you were talking and you said you're in your mother's womb, I saw myself sitting in her womb, and she was sitting at a table."

Marie went on to describe her mother's Bronx apartment

in great detail, especially the kitchen, where her aunt and mother were sitting, drinking tea and eating the special Italian cookies that her aunt always made for the Christmas holidays. Marie also seemed surprised that the Christmas tree was already up and decorated, since Christmas was still two weeks away.

The conversation between Marie's mother and aunt had turned very serious.

"While she was sitting there having a cup of tea," Marie continued, "I saw her and my aunt . . . and I was naturally in the womb there . . . and she said to my aunt: 'I'm going to die, and I'm not going to raise this girl child.'"

Incredulous, Marie explored the memory. Carefully, she described her thoughts as she watched and listened from the womb.

"And I said to myself, 'This is *weird*.' . . . My mother did die. . . . This was about a week or two before Christmas. . . . My mother did die on the fourteenth of January from pneumonia." Marie paused, then look up excitedly. "Now I can't wait to go home to call my aunt to ask her 'Was she sitting there and did she say this to you?' I'm sure she will remember and she's going to think I'm *nuts*, but this is what I saw the two ladies doing . . . and I never knew this before."

Marie had never been in her mother's old apartment after her birth, nor had her aunt told her about this conversation. Her aunt could, however, be counted on to remember exactly what was said. According to Marie, the eighty-year-old woman was "sharp as a tack."

Within two hours, Marie reported back. She had contacted her aunt, who confirmed everything.

"I called her and I said 'Aunt Marie, it's Cookie.' She said, 'Who the hell died now?' I said nobody died, but I'm going to talk fast, and you just listen to me. And I told her I want to know . . . were you at the table with my mother with the plate of cookies and the Christmas tree was up in the—"

Her aunt had cut her off. "Who the hell told you?" she demanded.

"I'm not even going to go into it to explain to you, but tell me what happened that day."

Marie's aunt said, "I came over with a hot plate of the cookies, which I made for your mother, which were her *favorite* cookies. And as she would eat 'em she rubbed her big fat belly, and she used to say 'This is for my little cookie.'"

"I have the nickname Cookie today," Marie explained. "Everybody calls me Cookie, because I love those things so much."

According to her aunt, Marie's mother had eaten two cookies, and stared at the Christmas tree. "Now this was two weeks before Christmas," Marie explained. "She put the tree up early because she thought I was going to be a Christmas baby."

Sitting at the table, the pregnant woman told her sister: "Marie, I'm not going to live to see this child raised. I will see her, and I know it will be a girl, and I want it named Rose Marie if I do not make it, but I *will* see her. I know that . . . but I know I'm going to die."

Aunt Marie had responded, "No, this is ridiculous!"

But Marie's mother was determined to have her say.

"Look at the Christmas tree and put a present under it every year for me, even though I'm not here," she continued.

Up to that point in the pregnancy, Marie's mother had been in excellent health. There was no physical reason to justify the ominous prediction.

"Lo and behold," her aunt had continued, "your mother had a little sniffle, that's all she had. Christmas day she came down with pneumonia. You had complications being born. Your mother died of lobar pneumonia, and you were born, and you survived."

"And it's absolutely true!" Marie told her aunt. Aunt Marie, meanwhile, continued to demand, "Who the hell told you?"

"I guess I can see and I can hear from the womb," Marie admitted. "*Now* I believe it." Her aunt's recollections had confirmed and enriched her own emotional and vivid experience.

Marie still had some questions for her aunt, and she was able to fill in even more blanks. She discovered that even her mother's kitchen and apartment were exactly as she had observed them.

Aunt Marie told her that she had named her according to her mother's instructions. She then repeated her dead sister's request to put presents under future Christmas trees.

"I asked, did you do it? And she said no!" We both smiled.

Vanessa is a young Hispanic woman who has had an incredibly difficult life thus far. Widowed after her husband succumbed to a sudden illness, she was having a difficult time coping with her grief. I met her at one of my large workshops, where I picked her at random from the audience to demonstrate an individual regression. As an audience of five hundred looked on expectantly, and her father watched anxiously, she went into a deep trance.

The important part of Vanessa's regression occurred in her mother's womb, in utero, before Vanessa's birth. In a deep state of relaxed concentration, she described the beautiful and peaceful light that permeated both her and the womb, providing a spiritual nourishment that complemented the nourishment of her mother's body. She could feel the love and welcome of her parents. At this moment, Vanessa's facial expression changed from a blissful state to one of astonishment and awe.

"I am aware of *everything*," she stated, "both inside and outside of the womb. . . . I know so much. . . . I can see and feel everything!"

Vanessa seemed to be stunned by the depth of her awareness from within her mother's womb. Her eyelids fluttered
under closed lids as she was silent. She later told me that in
that moment she was observing many things. Later her father
would confirm details of scenes she had glimpsed before her
birth.

"I can see ahead. . . . I can see the events of my life to
come. . . . They have a purpose; they are not the accidents I
thought," she said firmly, shifting to a higher perspective.

As she experienced the light, the sense of heightened
awareness, and the recognition of her life's plan and destiny,
the grief she had been carrying around began to lift. Her life
was being transformed in the present time, through memories
and experiences rooted in her own in-utero experience.

Memories from the in-utero period are important for many
reasons. They promote clinical improvements in patients
whose symptoms derived from early childhood traumas and
relationships. In addition, these memories demonstrate that an
actively engaged consciousness exists *before* birth, that the fetus
and infant are aware of so much more than we thought. They
are perceiving and integrating a great deal of information. In
light of this knowledge, we should rethink how we interact
with these tiny beings. They are keenly tuned into the expressions of love that we communicate to them, through words,
thoughts, and feelings.

In the second day of the workshops, one of those strangely
simultaneous life events occurred before the entire group.
Again I picked a volunteer to demonstrate an individual regression, this time using a more rapid type of hypnotic induction.

Ana, the volunteer patient, had missed the previous day because of an illness. Nobody had told her about the regression
with Vanessa.

Slipping quickly and deeply into the trance state, Ana also

went back to the in-utero period. She began to describe the beautiful golden-white light, her awareness of events both inside and outside her mother's body and her own, the reasons she was choosing these parents and this coming life, and how her life would be structured to best accomplish her soul's objectives.

I was amazed. Even though I occasionally encounter such simultaneous, or synchronous, events in my work, I am still always surprised by their statistical improbability.

The entire audience was stunned. Only Ana was unaware that what was transpiring was the nearly exact repetition of the previous day's regression with Vanessa.

Perhaps the group needed to hear the message twice that we are not here by some coincidence of nature. We are divine beings, enrolled for a while in this planetary school, and we have devised our curriculum in order to enhance the learning process. We are from the light, yet we are of the light, and we are so much wiser than we could ever imagine. All we need to do is to remember.

Amazing Childhood Memories

There are seven planes . . . seven through which we must pass before we are returned. One of them is the plane of transition. There you wait. In that plane it is determined what you will take back with you into the next life.

We are born with a considerable memory of our true home, the other side, that beautiful dimension that we have just left in order to enter a physical body once again. We are born with a tremendous capacity to receive and to give love, to experience pure joy, and to experience the present moment fully. As babies we do not worry about the past or the future. We feel and live spontaneously and completely in the moment, as we were meant to experience this physical dimension.

The assault on our minds begins when we are very young children. We are indoctrinated with parental, societal, cultural, and religious values and opinions that suppress our inborn knowledge. Should we resist this onslaught, we are threatened with fear, guilt, ridicule, criticism, and humiliation. Ostracism, withdrawal of love, or physical and emotional abuse may also loom.

Our parents, our teachers, our society, and our culture can and often do teach us dangerous falsehoods. Our world is evidence of this, as it staggers recklessly toward irreversible destruction.

If we allow them, children can show us the way out.

There is a well-known story in which a mother enters her infant's room and finds her four-year-old child hovering over the baby's crib.

"You must tell me about heaven and about God," the toddler implores his sibling. "I am beginning to forget!"

We have much to learn from our children before they do forget. In this life and in all of our others, we too have been children. We have remembered, and we have forgotten, and to save ourselves and to save our world now we must remember again. We must courageously overcome the brainwashing that has caused us so much grief and despair. We must reclaim our capacity for love and for joy. We must become fully human once again, as we were when we were young.

A mother whose son is now in his twenties told me about her son's strange behavior when he was three. The family's dog had just died, and she left her son with the dog as she went into the next room to phone the veterinarian to make arrangements for the dog's body.

When she returned, a stunning sight awaited her.

"I come into the room, and he has the dog all wrapped . . . his feet are wrapped with Band-Aids and butter. He's buttered the dog all the way. . . . All over the head and the tail and then he's wrapped the whole dog . . . dead dog . . . with all this stuff. I said, 'My God, what are you doing?'"

Her son answered, "Mommy, I'm making sure that she slides into heaven faster."

"And I thought," she continued, "oh, that's something he must have seen on *Sesame Street* or whatever. . . .

"I mentioned this some years later, before I knew about past lives, to a friend who said very nonchalantly over a cup of tea, 'Oh, he must have been an Egyptian. . . . That's what they did when their dogs died. . . . In a past life he was an Egyptian, and he buried his dog wrapped in oil and bandages.'"

The next day her friend brought over a book depicting the burial practices of the ancient Egyptians.

"When she showed me the picture in the book she brought me the next day, it was *exactly* what our dog looked like. . . . It was scary. I asked my son if he remembered doing that with the dog . . . and he said he did. And he said that the minute she died he knew that's what he had to do. . . . He had to go take care of her because her soul was just above her body. He understood this at three years old and went to work."

She concluded, "I am convinced now that he was an Egyptian, which is great because we're Jewish, and it's a nice blending of our cultures."

The writer Carey Williams told me about another fascinating case, this one of two-year-old twin boys living in New York City. Their father was a prominent physician. One day, he and his wife observed the twins speaking a strange language to each other, a language more sophisticated than the ones toddlers often invent. Rather than using made-up words for familiar objects, like television or telephone, these twins were speaking a much more complete vernacular. Their parents had never heard these words.

They brought the boys to the linguistics department of Columbia University, where a professor of ancient languages identified their "baby talk" as Aramaic. Aramaic is a virtually extinct language, now spoken only in a remote area of Syria. This ancient Semitic language was primarily spoken in the environs of Palestine, around the time of Christ.

You cannot pluck such an ancient tongue from late-night cable television, even in New York. You can, however, retrieve this knowledge from your past-life memory banks. Children are especially adept at this.

For example, you can ask your young child if he or she remembers when they were "big" before. Listen to the answer because it may be more than the product of an active imagination. Your child may actually provide details of a past life.

Observing the joy and spontaneity of children at play is always rewarding. Many of us have forgotten how to have fun and enjoy the simple pleasures of life. We worry too much about concepts such as success and failure, what kind of impression we are making on others, and about the future. We have forgotten how to play and have fun, and our children can remind us.

They remind us of our earliest values, of those things that are also really important in life: joy, fun, mindfulness of the present moment, trust, and the value of good relationships.

Our children have so much to teach us.

Karma and Lessons

We have debts that must be paid. If we have not paid out these debts, then we must take them into another life . . . in order that they may be worked through. You progress by paying your debts. Some souls progress faster than others. If something interrupts your ability . . . to pay that debt, you must return to the plane of recollection, and there you must wait until the soul you owe the debt to has come to see you. And when you both can be returned to physical form at the same time, then you are allowed to return. But you determine when you are going back. You determine what must be done to pay that debt.

There will be many lifetimes . . . to fulfill all of the agreements and all of the debts that are owed.

I have not yet been told about many of the other planes, but this plane, involving "debts that must be paid," evokes the concept of karma. Karma is an opportunity to learn, to practice love and forgiveness. Karma is also an opportunity for atonement, to wipe the slate clean, to make up to those we may have wronged or hurt in the past.

Karma is not only an Eastern concept. It is a universal idea, embodied in all the great religions (see "Responsibility for One's Actions" in Appendix A, "Shared Spiritual Values"). The Bible says, "What you sow, that is what you reap." Every thought and every action has inevitable consequences. We are responsible for our actions.

The surest way to reincarnate in a particular race or religion is to be manifestly prejudiced against that group. Hate is the express train carrying you to that group. Sometimes a soul learns to love by becoming what it most despised.

It is important to remember that karma is about learning, not about punishment. Our parents and the other people with whom we interact possess free will. They can love and help us or they can hate and harm us. Their choice is not your karma. Their choice is a manifestation of their free will. They are also learning.

Sometimes a soul will choose a particularly challenging lifetime in order to accelerate its spiritual progress, or as an act of love to help, guide, and nourish others who are also going through a similarly difficult lifetime. A hard life is not a punishment, but rather an opportunity.

We change races, religions, sex, and economic advantage because we must learn from all sides. We experience everything. Karma is ultimate justice. Nothing is overlooked or missed in our learning.

Grace, however, can supersede karma. Grace is divine intervention, a loving hand reaching down from the heavens to help us, to ease our burden and our suffering. Once we have learned the lesson, there is no need for further suffering, even if the karmic debt has not been fully repaid.

We are here to learn, not to suffer.

Elisabeth Kübler-Ross, the internationally famous psychiatrist and author whose pioneering research into death and dying and the NDE changed the way we deal with death, told me the following story.

Elisabeth was born an underweight triplet and the doctor told her mother that at least two of the babies would not survive. But Elisabeth's mother was a woman of exceptional strength and courage, a woman who freely gave anything and everything to others but refused anything in return, a proud and extremely self-reliant individual. She vowed that all three daughters would survive. She nursed them for nearly a year, keeping them with her in bed at all times for body warmth, like a present-day neonatal incubator. All three children survived and flourished.

Elisabeth was on the faculty of the University of Chicago Department of Psychiatry when she visited her mother in Switzerland, the family home. Her mother had an unusual request.

"Elisabeth, if I become a vegetable, I want you to give me something to put me out of my misery," her mother said.

"I can't do that," Elisabeth quickly replied.

"Yes, you can," her mother insisted. "You're the only one of my children who is a physician. You can give me something."

"No, I can't do that!" Elisabeth repeated. "Besides, people like you, you've always been healthy, hiking and climbing, you'll live to be ninety and go like that," Elisabeth added, snapping her fingers.

Elisabeth refused to discuss the subject of any assisted suicide further, and she returned to Chicago.

A month or so after this visit, Elisabeth's mother suffered a severe stroke that paralyzed most of her body. Although her mind remained relatively intact, this proud and independent woman had to rely on others for most basic needs.

"I learned to listen to the premonitions of others," Elisabeth told me.

Her mother died four years later, never having regained physical functioning. Elisabeth was furious with God.

Working with dying children and their remarkable drawings, Elisabeth's spiritual horizons were expanding despite her anger. She also had begun to meditate.

One day, soon after her mother's death, Elisabeth was "rocked" by a strong inner voice or message during her meditation.

"Why are you so angry at me?" the voice asked.

In her mind, Elisabeth replied, "Because you made my mother suffer so much: This beautiful, caring person who never accepted anything for herself but would give everything to others. You made her suffer for four years and then she dies!"

"That was a gift to your mother," the voice answered gently, "a gift of grace. Love must be balanced. If nobody were to receive love, who could give it? Your mother learned this in only four years, instead of coming back for one or several lifetimes severely retarded or physically impaired where she would *have* to accept the love of others. She has learned, and now she can move on."

Hearing this and understanding the message, Elisabeth let go of her anger. Understanding can immediately heal our deepest pain.

A mother and her teenage daughter participated in a group regression at one of my workshops, and both were overcome with emotion. During a break after the group exercise had been completed, they began to tell each other about their memories and reactions. They were startled to find themselves sharing the same lifetime, long ago and in more violent times.

"My daughter and I are here today," the mother reported to the group because her daughter was still too overwhelmed to speak, "and I'm pretty sure we had a piece of past-life recall which was the same life . . . during the meditation. What she told was that she just kept experiencing . . . she thought . . . being hit by a bull . . . or a man with bull's horns . . . and could see the horns. She kept getting hit again and again. . . ."

The mother continued, now talking about her own simultaneous experience. "When she first told me I just heard the getting hit by a bull and started to spin out. The piece that I got in my past life turned out to be almost a Viking. There were like skins and stuff and one of those heavy things on my head with those horns . . . and I came into a cave or a hut and this little kid came at me, and I killed him with a sword. And there was a lot of fear and it was all dark . . . and my daughter said that she was really afraid too . . . and her body hurt during the meditation, exactly where the sword wound was!"

She added, "It really . . . clearly . . . it's hard to talk about . . . much harder than I thought." Both mother and daughter were still experiencing a profound emotional reaction to their shared memories of that lifetime.

I pointed out that if this really were a shared lifetime they both spontaneously and simultaneously remembered, then they had died before and now they were here again, healthy and together. There was no need for any guilt or anger, only for forgiveness and love. Their shared memories and shared lifetimes demonstrated that there is no death, only life.

"Some of the healing part," I told them, "is not just the memory, not just the catharsis, but also the realization about death. And when you have it, and it's that intense, you start to realize that there is no death other than leaving the body. It's like walking through a door. But you are back again so you can make up, and you don't have to feel guilty—"

The mother interrupted me. "No, I don't . . . One of the things I've always told her is that I have liked her fierceness, even as a little kid. It has always really impressed me. We were joking about it now, and she said, 'Last time it got me killed!' But our relationship now feels very good, even better, and this whole thing feels . . . pretty powerful!"

❧ CHAPTER FOUR ❧

Creating Loving Relationships

There are different levels of learning, and we must learn some of them in the flesh. We must feel the pain. When you're a spirit you feel no pain. It is a period of renewal. Your soul is being renewed. When you're in physical state in the flesh, you can feel pain; you can hurt. In spiritual form you do not feel. There is only happiness, a sense of well-being. But it's a renewal period for . . . us. The interaction between people in the spiritual form is different. When you are in physical state . . . you can experience relationships.

After our birth in the physical state, our main source of learning is through relationships. Through the joy and pain of interaction with other people, we progress on our spiritual paths in order to learn about love from all sides. Relationships are a living laboratory, a field test to determine how we are doing, whether our lessons have been learned, to discover how close we are to our pre-determined life plan. In relationships our emotions are evoked, and we react. Have we learned to turn the other cheek, or do we retaliate with violence? Do we reach out to others with understanding, love, and compassion, or do we react with fear, selfishness, or rejection? Without relationships we would not know; we could not test our progress. They are wonderful but difficult opportunities to learn.

We are here in physical state in order to learn and to grow. We learn traits and qualities such as love, non-violence, compassion, charity, faith, hope, forgiveness, understanding, and awareness. We must unlearn negative traits and qualities, including fear, anger, hatred, violence, greed, pride, lust, selfishness, and prejudice.

It is primarily through relationships that we learn these lessons.

More learning can occur when there are many obstacles than when there are few or none. A life with difficult relationships, filled with obstacles and losses, presents the most opportunity for the soul's growth. You may have chosen the more difficult life so that you could accelerate your spiritual progress.

Sometimes a negative event, such as losing a job, may be the hand opening the door to a much better opportunity. We should not grieve prematurely. Destiny may need a little more time to weave its intricate tapestry. In addition to pain and hardship, there is also love and joy and ecstasy in this world. We are here to be in community, learning about love by being amidst other human beings who are on the same path, learning the same lessons. Love is not an intellectual process but rather a dynamic energy flowing into and through us at all times, whether we are aware of it or not. We must learn to receive love as well as to give. Only in community, only in relationships, only in service can we truly understand the all-encompassing energy of love.

Over many years I have treated countless couples and families who had been suffering in their relationships. I regressed some of them, and we often found the past-life causes of their current-day conflicts. Others needed better skills in communicating, and others needed to understand each other at deeper levels. Some needed to revise their values and priorities. And some needed a technique or two to help them climb out of their ruts, to become unstuck and begin to change. Which type of intervention they needed became clear to us over a brief period of time.

Growth occurred and their relationships were enriched when they honestly tried. Many of the suggestions and techniques I use with my patients are based on a deeper and more spiritual understanding of our lives and destinies than are the assumptions of traditional psychotherapy. I have found that our hearts and our souls yearn for and respond to psychospiritual therapy much more than they do to purely intellectual or mechanical approaches.

Because relationships are the soil of our growth while we are in physical state, I offer you some of my thoughts, suggestions, and techniques to help you in your relationships, especially if you feel some difficulty in this area of your life.

Many of these thoughts and ideas came to me one day while I was meditating in the foothills above the city of Medellín in Colombia. I value them highly because they arrived in my consciousness during meditation and I could sense the presence or at least the influence of the Masters around me, and thus I have barely edited this advice. I realize some may seem didactic and difficult. They were received, however, amidst a tremendous energy of caring and compassion. In reality, the messages and information are filled with love and healing. I can tell you from my experience in using these principles with those patients who needed help with their relationships that these techniques *really* work wonders.

The following ideas are presented to you in a brief and crystallized form, and are not designed for speed-reading. You may want to take some extra time to think about or to meditate upon those suggestions that apply to you or those that stir some kind of inner resonance. You might want to put your reflections of these ideas into your journal.*

There is no hurry, there is no schedule, there is no test, and there certainly is no competition between you and your partner, whether your partner is your lover, your parent, your child, your friend, or any other with whom you are in a relationship.

I hope these help you to love more freely and without fear.

Increasing Your Awareness of Self and Other

What is revealed to me is what is important to me, what concerns me. Each person must be concerned with him- or herself . . . with making him- or herself . . . whole. We have lessons to learn . . . each one of us. They must be learned one at a time . . . in order. Only then can we know what the next person needs, what he or she lacks or what we lack, to make us whole.

Understand the nature of the self, the Real Self, which is immortal. This understanding will help you keep things in the proper perspective.

Know yourself, so that you can see clearly, without the distortions of the conscious mind or the subconscious. Practice meditation and visualization, detached observation, peaceful perception, feeling a sense of detached loving-kindness or loving detachment. Cultivate this state.

Know your thoughts and assumptions, and realize that you may have swallowed them whole. When you generalize into

---

*I have supplemented some of the techniques with suggestions from the book *I Will Never Leave You*, by Hugh and Gayle Prather.

groups or stereotypes, you stop seeing the unique individual. Erroneous assumptions from our past such as "Men are brutish and insensitive" or "Women are *too* sensitive and emotional" lead to a distorted reality. Experience is much stronger than belief. Learn from your experiences. What helps without harming is valuable. Discard outdated beliefs and thoughts.

Happiness comes from within. It is not dependent on external things or on other people. You become vulnerable and can be easily hurt when your feelings of security and happiness depend on the behavior and actions of other people. Never give your power to anyone else.

Try not to become attached to things. In the three-dimensional world we learn through relationships, not things. We all know that you cannot take things with you when you leave.

When we die and our souls progress to higher dimensions, we take our behaviors, our deeds, our thoughts, and our knowledge with us. How we treated others in relationships is infinitely more important than what we have accumulated materially. Also, we may gain and lose many material objects during the course of our lifetime. You will not meet your possessions in the afterlife, but you will meet your loved ones. This thought should help you to rethink your values if necessary.

Men Are from Mars, Women Are from Venus, by John Gray, has been a best-seller for many years in many countries. Numerous other books, movies, and television shows also have emphasized the seemingly insurmountable differences between men and women. A vast gulf separates the sexes and is apparent in the way we think and how we behave. We don't see the world the same way. Testosterone, the male hormone, inclines men toward aggression and competition instead of cooperation, toward "ownership" of home territory and of family. Estrogen and progesterone, the female hormones, seem to foster sensitivity, communication rather than competition, less urge toward aggression and more toward protection.

The way boys and girls are raised compounds the inborn asymmetry and adds to the biological walls separating men and women. Boys are socially encouraged to be more aggressive, more competitive, more assertive. Girls are taught to be more passive, more communicative, more cooperative. We are taught different values by our parents and teachers, by our society and culture, and by our media and advertisers.

There seems to be a great deal of truth to all of this. No problem can be solved until an awareness of this problem bubbles into consciousness. So now we know. What comes next?

Certainly, boys can and should be raised to become aware of and to express more sensitivity. They can be taught to be more cooperative, and they can learn better communication skills. Girls can be raised to be more confident and more assertive. Overall, the raising of boys needs to be altered more than the raising of girls, because the world is engulfed today by the violence caused almost exclusively by men.

But what about the inborn biological differences? How can we change biology? What do we do about testosterone? Here is one metaphor.

Hormones and certain genetic factors cause hair to grow on the faces of men. Does this mean that beards are inevitable, that all men need to walk around with long beards on their faces?

Of course the answer is no. Men have the option to shave off their beards. Any man can choose to do this or not.

The biological influences are tendencies. They can be overcome by the conscious will. Testosterone and other hormones impel, but they do not compel. Just as men can choose to shave, they can choose to be non-violent, less aggressive, more cooperative and communicative, more sensitive.

The conscious decision by men to choose the loving path, not the violent path, is the next step.

Beyond this choice lies yet another step, which is the re-awakening to the spiritual truth that we are spirit and soul, not body and brain. The soul has no sex, no hormones, no biological tendencies. The soul is pure, loving energy.

As we become aware of our spiritual nature, we recognize our true essence. We are immortal and divine. Renouncing violence, hate, dominance, selfishness, and ownership of people and things becomes even easier with this recognition. Accepting love, compassion, charity, hope, faith, and cooperation becomes the natural thing to do.

Some switching of the sexes occurs over the course of our many lifetimes. We have all been men, and we have all been women. Although I believe we tend to specialize in one sex or the other, we all must, like college students, take some elective courses as the other sex. We have to learn from all sides. Rich and poor. Strong and weak. Buddhist, Christian, Jewish, Hindu, Muslim, or other religions. Different races. And, of course, man and woman.

And so we all can eventually learn to overcome any negative biological tendencies in order to manifest our spiritual nature fully. Similarly, we all can learn to overcome any negative social or cultural teaching for the same reason.

Some will lag behind, because even though we are all traveling on the same path, we are not all progressing at the same speed. It is the job of those ahead to reach back, with compassion and with love, to help those behind.

To reach back and help, and expect neither reward nor even thanks.

To reach back and help, because that is what spiritual beings do.

★   ★   ★

I vividly remember being rescued by Marianne Williamson, a wonderful author and speaker, when we were presenting a workshop on healing relationships. The format was a dialogue. Marianne and I had agreed that I would talk for ten minutes, then she would talk for ten minutes, and then we would open the dialogue to the audience, answering and discussing their questions, for the next hundred minutes. There were about eight hundred people in the audience.

Approximately five minutes into my opening comments, a woman near the front of the room stood up and raised her hand. Her behavior distracted me, and I asked what she wanted.

Somewhat angrily, she said, "I came here for a dialogue, not a list!" I had begun my ten-minute talk by going through a brief list of suggestions that I had used with my patients when I did couples therapy in my office. These techniques really helped people, and I was sharing my "list" with the group. Of course, this woman did not know I was only going to talk for ten minutes. Perhaps she feared my list would expand to fill the entire two hours.

I began to open my mouth to explain how Marianne and I had agreed to structure the time. But I never got a chance to say a word.

Marianne, immediately protecting me, had jumped up, walked behind me and, with her hands firmly on my shoulders, glared at the woman standing alone in a room of eight hundred people.

"Don't you know that men make lists!" Marianne answered in a firm voice. The woman slumped back into her seat. "Why are you negating him? Why are you taking this away from him?"

Then Marianne launched into an eloquent and passionate speech about the differences between men and women.

I appreciated Marianne's defense. Perhaps men do make

lists, I agreed, although some women do also. And women tend to rescue, as Marianne demonstrated, I thought silently to myself.

Love yourself. Do not worry about the opinions of others. If you really need to and want to decline some offer or obligation, say so. If you fail to do so, anger will creep in. You will resent the commitment, and you will resent the person who obligated you. It is better to say no when you need to, and to say yes when you want to. Physical illness often follows when one is not able to decline unwanted commitments, because this is a more "acceptable" way of saying no. Then you have no choice but to decline because your body says no for you. It is much healthier to assert yourself. There is a saying that I've seen on a T-shirt that sums it up in a humorous way: Stress is when your mind says no, but your mouth opens up and says yes.

Projection is the psychological action of denying your fear and unconscious motivations and then giving these fears and motives to others. Be careful not to project your hidden feelings onto another or to ascribe motives and intent when there are none. This distortion of reality harms both you and the other.

For example, if you have fears of abandonment and low self-esteem and your date doesn't show up at the restaurant for your dinner reservation, you may tell yourself: "He really doesn't care about me; he's standing me up because someone better came along." In reality, your date may have been stuck in traffic.

Understand the nature and influence of repeating patterns, from childhood experiences or even from past lives. Without understanding, patterns tend to repeat, unnecessarily damaging the relationship.

★　　　★　　　★

In my previous books, I have described how to recognize these repeating patterns and how to differentiate past-life from present-life origins. In Chapter Two of this book, the reaction of Andrea's mother to her newborn son's illness reflects a past-life pattern (reaction to loss) repeating in the current life. Patterns of turning to alcohol or drugs in order to cope often have been repeating over many lifetimes.

In relationships, as with alcohol and drugs, old patterns such as dominance, manipulation, or abuse may have once again resurfaced and be negatively affecting the participants.

Sometimes regression to childhood or to past lives can show the real roots of an issue. Other times the roots are shallow, arising from this life, and we are only letting our pride stand in the way of resolution.

One of the most important of life's lessons is to learn independence, to understand freedom. This means independence from attachments, from results, from opinions, and from expectations. Breaking attachments leads to freedom, but breaking attachments does not mean abandoning a loving and meaningful relationship, a relationship that nourishes your soul. It means ending *dependency* on any person or thing. Love is never a dependency.

Love is an absolute, unconditional, and timeless state that asks for nothing in return.

Since it is important to love and honor yourself, you should not remain in a destructive relationship, even if you feel that you love the other person. The connection with that person might not work because of your partner's problems, lack of understanding, or exercise of free will, but it is important to remember that love is timeless. You will have many more chances to get it right.

See the other person clearly, and don't put that person on a pedestal. Your parents, your teachers, your authority figures are just people like you. They have their own fears, doubts, anxieties, and imperfections. They also have their own agendas, and sometimes you are a pawn in their games. See them as equals, as your brothers and sisters. Their judgments carry no extra weight. Consider their opinions. They may be wise. They may be right. But they may also be wrong.

In my workshops I often tell the story of a patient whose father was an aloof, distant, and authoritarian man. He was a judge, and he demanded a high pedestal for himself, not only from the people who appeared before him in court, but also from his wife and children.

He could never hug his daughter, nor could he tell her that he loved her.

After he died, she felt that her relationship with her father was unfinished, unresolved, but she could not see him clearly; the pedestal was too high.

One day, in a deeply relaxed state, my patient visualized herself in a beautiful garden. There, her father, younger and much healthier than in his declining days, appeared to her.

"Think of me as your brother," he lovingly instructed.

Those words changed the whole tenor of their relationship. She could now see her father as an equal, no longer a superior. She could see both his virtues and his flaws much more clearly and comfortably.

She could understand him and forgive him.

She had been sustaining the pedestal, but now that pedestal disappeared, as did the distortion of reality that projection always causes.

Love and forgiveness filled the vacuum.

Often we take personally the slings and arrows of our "abusers." But frequently we are merely the interchangeable pawns of their own neurotic dramas. Anyone else in your position would have received the same treatment. There is nothing especially noxious or negatively noteworthy about you.

Beware of the packaging people come in. The most dangerous people often wear the most alluring packaging: exciting, fun, impulsive, risky, living on the edge. Often these outer traits blind your heart's eyes, and you do not see the danger. Learn to see with your heart, not your eyes.

Denial, the act of not being aware of inner feelings and fears and motivations, is the opposite of mindfulness. You can say and do things that can damage the relationship. When you are awakened, when you truly know yourself, you will not inadvertently hurt the other person.

Promoting Love and Understanding in the Relationship

When you look into the eyes of another, any other, and you see your own soul looking back at you, then you will know you have reached another level of consciousness.

Relationships need nurturing and attention. Detach from your fears and negative emotions. When you need to talk or communicate, reset your priorities. Devote time and energy to the other person. Bring your full awareness and attention to the relationship and its problems. The relationship is more important than that television, magazine, or newspaper. Eliminate distractions. Turn off the television; put down the newspaper. Respect the other person.

Do not take anything for granted. Do not stay in your rut. Renew the relationship through loving actions. The relationship is living, alive in the present. It is not a thing of the past.

Allow the soul to enter the relationship through awareness

and understanding. This promotes an alchemy to deeper processes: soul/right brain in harmony with ego/left brain. Soulful relationships bring true joy into our lives.

It is safe to love completely, without holding back. You can never be truly rejected. It is only when the ego is involved that we feel bruised and vulnerable. Love itself is absolute and all-encompassing. The concept of loving completely and without reservation may seem risky or even dangerous to many. I am not, however, talking about self-abrogation in a relationship, nor enduring a relationship that is abusive or damaging. Doing so is not loving to yourself or to the other. Staying in a destructive relationship is *not* an example of loving without reservation—instead it may be more a manifestation of low self-esteem and lack of self-love than anything else. People can be dangerous, but love is not.

Reach out with love and compassion to help others without concern for what you may gain. Whether you reach out to a few or to many is not important. The numbers do not matter; the act of reaching out with caring does. Sometimes when a physician touches a patient with compassion and healing, the physician benefits more than the patient. All of us are physicians of the soul.

Come from the heart, the true heart, not the head. When in doubt, choose the heart. This does not mean to deny your own experiences and that which you have empirically learned through the years. It means to trust your self to integrate intuition and experience. There is a balance, a harmony to be nurtured, between the head and the heart. When the intuition rings clear and true, loving impulses are favored.

The more you practice listening to that calm inner voice, intuition, or "gut feeling," the more accurate and clear the voice will become.

Trust. You can trust in love. Individual decisions may appear harmful, but love is not. When the bigger picture is grasped and appreciated, the loving intent becomes clear. Your child may not understand that the antibiotic injection is a loving act. You are concerned and will spare nothing to protect your child from a potentially dangerous illness. In the child's mind, however, the injection may appear to be a hurtful act. In a more complex scenario, you may have to send a loved one away because the relationship is destructive, or his or her drug problem demands hospitalization for the person's own safety, against his or her will. These are just examples of the necessity for grasping the overall picture before judging the individual decision or actions.

Like many other men, I tend to think that romantic gestures have to be of the grand sort, such as jewelry, flowers, a big night out, and the like. However, I have learned that sometimes the smallest things can mean the most.

Many years ago, I was resident in psychiatry in Connecticut. Our son, Jordan, was a toddler at the time, and Carole worked on a part-time basis. Often I had to work late at the hospital. On one extremely hot summer night, I left the hospital at around eleven at night. On a whim, I stopped and bought two ice cream cones, one for Carole and one for me, and brought them home. Carole and I had not had a chance to talk to each other so I had no idea that it had been a particularly trying day for her, both at work and at home. We sat and ate the ice cream and shared some time together in the quiet of the evening. She has told me that my thinking about her and bringing her that cone has always been a favorite loving memory of hers.

Help the other along her life's plan and goals. Security in a relationship comes from present, loving actions.

End dependency. Do not take away self-esteem, money, or confidence in order to make someone dependent on you. Do not diminish anyone. People do not leave truly loving relationships unless they are unaware.

In Carole's family there is a saying that has come down through the years that the greatest sin is to take away someone's *neshumah*. Translated from the Yiddish, the expression means that it is a sin to take away another's joy, or, more colloquially, to rain on someone's parade. How frequently people do that to each other and how destructive it is! We've all had that happen, and we've all had the sinking feeling that goes with it. Children who are proud of a drawing or of singing a song or of some other small accomplishment are met with laughter instead of a pat on the back. Later in life, we sometimes find our moments of happiness ruined by someone's criticism. Even though we know that the other person's actions and words are due to jealousy or feelings of inferiority or any number of reasons, we still have that unhappy feeling that we had as a child. It is interesting to note that the word *neshumah* actually means "soul." The greatest sin is to take away someone's soul.

The following tips offer ways to communicate in a more compassionate and less judgmental manner. They actually are mini-exercises, and if you practice these techniques often, your relationships should improve, if not prosper. Once again, take your time, because the suggestions are crystallized. And feel free to be creative, to modify these techniques and suggestions as you see fit.

For example, role-switching can evolve into a more formalized process where you allow yourself to reach a deeper level of relaxed concentration and try to project yourself *into* the other person's mind. Try to be the other person, to understand his or her reactions, his or her fears and hopes and joys. This process can take as long as you need. There is no time limit.

Give positive verbal messages. Hold hands more often.

Compliment from the heart. All of us need to receive love as well as to give love.

Try to communicate without criticism, without judgment, without any intent to hurt or harm. Communicate your love and caring and compassion. Do not communicate to harm or to win.

Put aside ego and pride, as they only get in the way. Listen carefully, with detachment and perspective. Make your shared space a sanctuary so the other can speak safely.

Do not speak until you have something to say, preferably something positive. Do not speak reflexively. It is always safer to be quiet, to listen, to understand. Determine the underlying fear or fears behind the thought or action. See the bigger picture, and do not get distracted by the anger or emotion. See the real issue, the underlying fear that is always lurking there behind the drama.

Never act or speak from anger. Words have a lasting effect and power, and they are not easily forgotten. Never let alcohol or drugs do the talking. You can never completely erase the wounds inflicted by words of anger or hate.

Winning an argument can be losing if ego is involved. Doing that which promotes love, understanding, and cooperation is true winning. If you promote negative thoughts and emotions: fear, anger, guilt, shame, sadness, anxiety, worry, and hate, either in yourself or your partner, then you have lost.

Letting go of anger is difficult. We feel justified, self-righteous, as if our integrity and honor are on the line, being tested. The only test in this great school we call humanity is whether we are learning to discharge anger and embrace love. Holding onto anger poisons our relationships. Continue to love, even if the other is angry, hurt, and fearful. Love is a constant; anger is transient.

Determine the causes of the anger, improve the conditions, and let go. How long does it take you to let go? Five days, three days, one day, one hour? If you always let go within five days, why not in one hour? You can do it.

A few years ago, I was treating a husband and wife in my office in couples therapy. This couple had intelligence and insight, and their relationship was overall fairly good. But their good times were too often interrupted by emotionally charged arguments, which inevitably led to angry and hurt feelings. They would hold onto their anger for days, each suffering miserably and each feeling very uncomfortable. Yet their pride prevented them from ending the siege earlier, from stopping their misery before it acquired a life of its own.

They came into my office once after a week-long feud. For seven straight days, the most minor of events caused the simmering anger to boil over.

After about thirty minutes of therapy with them, the issues were resolved and their anger had just about dissipated. As usual, pride and hurt feelings had prolonged their angry quarrel, preventing an early resolution.

I tried a new approach.

"In these fights of yours . . . fights which *always* are ended sooner or later," I pointed out, "how long does it usually take for you to get over your anger and make up?"

"Well, usually about five or six days," the husband answered. His wife agreed.

"Do you think you could do it in three days?" I asked. "That would still give you plenty of time to fight and stew and work things out. If you can do this in five days, why not in three? You always end the fight anyway."

They both thought for a moment and then nodded their approval. Sure, they could fight for only three days instead of five or six.

"Well," I went on, "if you could make up in three days, why not in one day? Surely you know the whole process of your fights, from the very start to the making up at the end. And you have learned all the tools necessary to resolve your differences. Can't you accelerate the process and do the whole thing in only one day?"

Again, they considered this proposal. Again, they agreed. One day would be enough.

"So," I continued, "how about six hours? Wouldn't that be enough? After all, if you can make up in one day, why not in six hours? Think of how much less misery and suffering you would have. Only six hours."

Again this concept made sense to them, and again they agreed.

I kept shortening the time span for their fights. Eventually I got them down to one or two hours. They would recognize the causes of the incipient fight and angry feelings, they would negotiate and compromise, and they would be empathic to the feelings of the other spouse. They would try to do all this in one hour or so.

Since that time, this abbreviated fight/anger/resolution process has always worked for this couple. They already had realized that they always ended their fights and anger anyway. And now, instead of suffering for five or six days, they only had to have a short period of misery.

We can all learn to compress our angry periods into early recognition and rapid resolution. Eventually we always let go of our anger. Why hold onto it and suffer needlessly?

Forgive the past. It is over. Learn from it and let go. People are constantly changing and growing. Do not cling to a limited, disconnected, negative image of a person in the past. See that person now. Your relationship is always alive and changing.

Begin actively loving the other right now. Do not grieve or regret not loving in the past. The past is over. Begin right now. It is never too late to express your love and compassion.

When I visited Brazil in 1996, a woman said to me, very upset, "I really feel terrible when I look back at the strict, authoritarian way I brought up my eldest son when he was little. I was very young and immature, and I simply raised him the way my mother raised me. I wish I could start over!"

I replied, "Love him now, the way you wish you had when he was a child."

When I returned to Brazil in 1997, I met her again. She was pleased with her own progress. Regular meditation had helped her break away from the affective paralysis imposed on her by guilt, drawing her closer to her son as she showered on him all the love and attention backed up within her.

Visualize even more. See the gulf between you and your partner fade away and fill with a beautiful energy. You are not icebergs floating separately, but you are the water that connects them. See and feel this connection. Send your light and love. At some level he or she will receive it. We are all connected to each other.

Carole and I conduct intensive training programs several times a year. During one of these classes, Carole worked with a man who discovered the essence of love.

From Carole:

People often ask me if I've discovered Brian in a prior lifetime. I've had regressions for help with certain problems, but I haven't specifically looked for a past life with him. There's been no reason other than just curiosity to experience a regression to find him. It's really unimportant to me because I've always felt a very profound love and connectedness between us. But this is a reason why people often want regressions, to see if someone significant in their life now is someone they had known in a prior lifetime. Arthur was one of these people.

It was the second day of one of our professional training

courses, and I had just finished a presentation. Arthur, a South African man in his sixties, approached me and asked if I would help him with a problem of his, one of the reasons he had come to the group. I told him that first he should work within the group for the next few days and see what progress could be made. I expected that the answers he was seeking would reveal themselves in the intense group and individual interactions.

On the fourth day Arthur came to me and said that while he had worked with other people there was still something that was troubling him. So while Brian was doing a large group exercise, Arthur and I went into another room, and we started to work on a one-to-one basis.

I asked Arthur what he wanted to accomplish. His beloved mother had died quite a while ago. He had four grandchildren, and although he loved all of them very much, one was particularly dear to him. He wondered if this little girl was his mother reincarnated.

We decided to go back to see if his subconscious could lead him to a prior lifetime when he and his mother were together. Arthur also told me that he was not very visual at all and he thought that some of the problems he was having during the week were due to that.

After a relatively short induction we went back in time, and Arthur found himself in the 1800s in England. He was a young boy standing outside. He could see the house that he lived in with his family, although he was not sure that they owned the house. I instructed him to go inside. He knew that there were people in the house who were his parents, but he could not get a very good look at them. He knew that he had siblings, but he could not get a good grasp on them, either.

So we went forward to a time when Arthur was going to a boarding school. Now he could see that he had a brother and a sister, but his parents were still quite hazy to him. Life was very good, and he was happy at the boarding school. He realized that his sister in that lifetime was his mother in this lifetime, and he was elated by this. He thought that his brother might be his son in this lifetime.

In time he became an attorney and we moved forward to his wedding day. Despite being concerned about his inability to use his visual senses, Arthur was able to see the scene in detail. At the wedding he could see that his sister and his brother were there. He could see that his parents were also present, but he could still not make out their faces. They were still not recognizable to him, nor was he concerned with them. He was just pleased to find his brother and sister.

The ceremony was lovely and Arthur was happy about the day. He explained that his marriage was one not of love, but of convenience. He had grown up with this girl, and their families had decided that it would be good for them to get together and get married. That was all right with him, she was a friend, and that was what was expected of him. In time they had several children and Arthur became a successful lawyer.

Moving still forward to the day he died, Arthur could see himself as an old man surrounded by his family, his wife and his children. He had led a very good life. He said that the marriage had developed into love. He cared for his wife deeply, and they and their children had been quite happy. We found no evidence of conflicts or traumas in that lifetime. Instead, we found an old man, fading away, who died surrounded by his loved ones.

Then, according to Arthur, he went into "what you in the States would call a tornado." He was passing into another dimension. There, Arthur could see loved ones, family and friends, waiting for him. He could see them, but he knew that he could not go to them until he first met with beings who asked him to review his life. He had to do that before he could move on. They asked him to look back on his life and to see what the theme of his life was, to determine what his life's lesson was. He took some time to consider that and then explained that the lesson had to do with not needing a great life or a momentous life or a life full of excitement or full of great happenings to be able to experience contentment and love and to give love to others. Arthur said the beings seemed to be pleased with that answer.

He was then able to join his family and friends: He was euphoric about that. He recognized several people. His brother was there. His parents were not there; they were somewhere else. They were not with his group. This was interesting because his parents in that life never were very definite to him. They were always very hazy.

I asked if he could see his sister. His eyes scanned under his lids, and he said, "No, she's not here." And then his face started to beam and he said, "Oh, she's coming now. Now I can see her. Yes, yes, she is part of us. She is with us."

After giving him some time to savor his happiness, I again asked what was going on. He told me, "Oh, we're waiting, we're waiting. It's just waiting now to decide when to go to be reincarnated, when to come back again."

I asked who was nearby, and he said there were Masters there. He said they were helping him figure out what he was going to do in his next life. Interestingly enough, he explained that the Masters were there to give advice only if he asked for advice; they did not impose themselves otherwise.

I inquired whether he could ask them questions about his life now. After a pause he said, "Yes, yes, that is possible." I suggested that he might see if they knew whether his granddaughter was the same soul as his beloved mother.

Arthur was quiet for a while. Finally, he said, "They have answered me. They said, 'Did you love your mother?' And I answered, 'Yes, I loved her very much.' And they asked again, 'Do you love your granddaughter?' And I said, 'Oh, I love her very, very much.' And the answer from the Masters was, 'Then what difference does it make? Does it really matter whether your granddaughter was your mother?' And I said, 'No, it doesn't matter at all. It's the love I feel for them, that's what matters. Love is love.' They seemed pleased with that answer."

Arthur emerged from this regression feeling extremely contented. He would search no more.

Our souls exist in an energetic stream of love. We are never truly separated from our loved ones, even though we may feel apart and unloved. Our reunions can be unexpected and dramatic.

Diane was my patient. She is a pretty woman in her mid-thirties, with short brown hair and hazel eyes. Although petite in size, she is powerful in her personality. As the head nurse of an urgent care unit in a large medical center, she has to make many life-and-death decisions daily, and she skillfully directs a large staff of nurses and technicians.

At the time, Diane was upset that she was thirty-five and not yet married. Some men she had dated were intimidated by her, and were not comfortable with her strong personality. Although several men had proposed to her, she had decided not to settle, not to marry unless love and passion were present in the relationship. She was looking for a soulmate, but apparently none had arrived. She also had vague feelings of guilt and unworthiness and sometimes felt she did not deserve to find love and to be happy.

During a vivid past-life regression, Diane found herself in North America a few hundred years ago during the Indian wars. She was a settler, a young mother with a toddler son. Her husband was away, and their cabin was surrounded by an Indian hunting party. She and the baby were hiding in a secret compartment built under the floor.

"My baby is between one and two years old. He has dark hair and brown eyes," she told me. "He's so cute," she added.

I was already experiencing a foreboding of tragedy as she described her baby and the scene.

"He has a birthmark beneath his right shoulder . . . it's in the shape of a half-full moon or curved sword," she continued. "I have long black hair and a simple cloth dress."

I brought her back to the hiding place, and, within moments, she began to sob. I directed her to float above the scene, to detach from it and to observe from above, as if she were watching a movie. In this manner I could help her to control her emotions while continuing to describe the past-life drama.

"I have to hide here or else they will kill us. This is our plan . . . but the baby's crying . . . he's crying. I have to hold my hand over his mouth . . . he just won't stop!" She became tearful again.

"He's dead. . . . I killed him. I didn't mean to . . . he wouldn't stop crying. Oh God, oh God, what have I done?"

The Indians did not find her, but the rest of her life was wracked with pain and guilt. She never forgave herself.

The woman went on to have two other children in that lifetime, and they and her grandchildren were at her deathbed at the end of that tragic life. Being a caring mother and grandmother had only slightly assuaged her guilt, shame, and self-punishment.

She died and floated above her body, describing a beautiful golden light in the shape of a circle. Within the circle she could see the spirits of her loved ones who had died before her, including her husband and parents. But her baby was not there.

Nevertheless, she finally felt an incredible peace. Music came from the light, but she could not find adequate words to describe it.

"The light and the music are so beautiful that there are no

words . . . no words to explain. It's like going home. They're greeting me. I am going home."

She felt a twinge of sadness at leaving her children and grandchildren, but the joy she was finding in the light and in the music was overwhelming.

"They don't understand that I am not dead, even though I have left my body. I am still aware, still conscious. Death is the wrong word. I haven't really died, but they don't know this."

She was right. We never really die. We just expand our level of consciousness, as if we were walking through a door into a brighter, more vivid environment, an environment animated by the light and the music of love.

Several months after this regression experience, Diane was at work in the hospital, examining a forty-one-year-old man who was experiencing intermittent asthma attacks. She felt inexplicably attracted to this man, but she mentally dismissed her attraction and continued the physical examination.

His eyes followed her carefully. He, too, was feeling some odd connection, almost a familiarity, with this pretty nurse. They were bantering with each other and discovered a great deal of common ground.

Since asthma was his presenting symptom, Diane walked around him to listen to his lungs. She placed her stethoscope on his back, more intent on listening than on looking. She nearly fainted. Her breath froze and her knees buckled when she saw the crescent-shaped birthmark beneath his right shoulder.

She knew immediately that some profound event was taking place.

Diane steered the conversation around to his marital status. Meanwhile, tears of joy were welling up in her eyes.

He was divorced. His wife had had several affairs during their marriage, and she had left him years ago. He felt hurt and betrayed, and his confidence had been damaged. He had not remarried, fearing that he would be betrayed once more. He could not bear to endure such pain again.

He thought to himself, Why am I telling this nurse such personal and intimate things? What is it about her?

I believe their meeting was not coincidental. Their love, their unfinished past-life relationship, and their life's plan had pulled them together again. Their souls had planned this meeting. They are now happily married.

Diane no longer has feelings of guilt or unworthiness. I never treated her husband, although I wanted to. My motive was not to validate their past-life connection. The soul recognition, the birthmark, their happiness together were enough. They were in love, and love needs no proof.

I wanted to help alleviate his asthma. For as I have described in my previous books, death from suffocation in previous lives often manifests as symptoms of asthma in this lifetime.

CHAPTER FIVE

Removing Obstacles to Happiness and Joy

You know so much more than the others. You understand so much more. Be patient with them. They don't have the knowledge that you have. Spirits will be sent back to help you. But you are correct in what you are doing . . . continue. This energy must not be wasted. You must get rid of the fear. That will be the greatest weapon you have.

We are all created in the image of God, and God is within us all. Our basic underlying nature is loving, peaceful, balanced, and harmonious. We are innately compassionate, caring, and kind. We are souls.

Over the course of our lifetimes, an overlay of fear, anger, envy, sadness, insecurity, and many other negative thoughts and emotions accrues and covers our beautiful inner nature. This outer covering is intensified and reinforced by our childhood training and experiences in the current life. We appear to be what we are not—angry and fearful people, filled with insecurity, guilt, and self-doubts. We have forgotten who we really are.

We do not need to learn about love and balance, about peace and compassion, about forgiveness and faith. We have always known these things.

Instead, our task is to *unlearn* those negative and harmful emotions and attitudes that plague our lives and cause us, our communities, and our world such misery. As we let go of these negative traits, lo and behold, we rediscover our true nature, our positive and loving self. It has been there all the time, covered over, obscured, and forgotten.

When we remove the outer layers of dirt and debris, the negative thoughts and emotions, when we clean and polish away the outer overlay, then we can once again discern the true diamonds we really are. We are immortal and divine souls on our way home. We have always been diamonds underneath.

Letting go of fear, anger, and other negative emotions is important for good physical health as well as for spiritual well-being. It is now widely recognized that mental stress (which includes negative emotions such as fear, anger, chronic anxiety, and depression) is one of the leading causes of illness and death in the world. Our bodies are intimately linked to our minds, so our moods and emotions are easily translated into physical symptoms. Love can heal; stress can kill.

The New England Journal of Medicine, overwhelmingly considered to be the best general medical journal in the United States, published a major article in January of 1998 detailing the multi-system damage that chronic stress can inflict on the human body.

This article reports that mental stress causes a complex system of hormones and other chemicals to be released in the body. When these hormones are not rapidly inactivated, when the stress persists and the body continues to produce these chemicals, many organs in our body are exposed to harmful consequences. Stress causes changes in heart rate, blood pressure, and blood-sugar levels, and it increases the secretion of cortisol, a powerful natural steroid hormone.

Stress also alters the secretion of gastric acid, adrenaline and other strong chemicals whose production should only be accelerated at specific, limited times. Perhaps worst of all, stress has been shown to depress the natural functioning of our immune system, impairing our ability to fight infections and chronic illnesses, such as cancer and AIDS.

The article concludes that chronic stress creates damaging physiological changes, and that among these problems can be insulin resistance, heart disease, memory loss, immune-system dysfunction, and decreased bone-mineral density (osteoporosis, which leads to weakness of bone and increased likelihood of fractures).

One of the medical researchers quoted in the article states, "Physicians and other health-care providers can help patients reduce [the risk of such stress-related problems] by helping them learn coping skills, recognize their own limitations, and relax."

Dean Ornish, M.D., the brilliant cardiologist who pioneered studies on the effects of stress on heart disease and prostate cancer and the author of the recently published book *Love & Survival: The Scientific Basis for the Healing Power of Intimacy*, has said, "[Opening the heart] has everything to do with not only the quality of our life, but also the quantity of our life—how long we live. . . . Loneliness and isolation increase the likelihood of disease and premature death from all causes by 200 to 500 percent or more. . . . When we're lonely we tend to over-eat, work too hard, drink too much, abuse drugs or engage in self-destructive behaviors like that."

According to Ornish, "Love and intimacy are at the root of what makes us sick and what makes us well, what causes sadness and what brings happiness, what makes us suffer and what leads to healing. . . . I am not aware of any other factor in medicine—not diet, not smoking, not exercise, not stress, not genetics, not drugs, not surgery—that has a greater impact on our quality of life, incidence of illness, and premature death from all causes."

On a personal note, Ornish has said that finding his own emotional health "wasn't about finding the right person, but *being* the right person."

To let go of negative thoughts and emotions and to discover inner peace, joy, and happiness—these are the goals. You will find life so much more enjoyable. You will progress with more awareness along your spiritual path. And your soul will manifest itself within a physical body that is infinitely more healthy and resistant to diseases. What a wonderful combination. Even if you are still debating or mulling over the spiritual lessons and implications, there is no doubt about the physical benefits you can obtain from the practices and attitudes described here. These health benefits present strong practical reasons for following the suggestions in this book. Along the way, spiritual benefits will accrue anyway. You have nothing to lose, and you have everything to gain.

Letting Go of Anger

Anger is rooted in judgment. We hold others to some standard that we have somehow fantasized, chosen, and applied to them. They may not even know about these standards, but that does not matter to us.

So often people are angry at us because we have not met their expectations. The expectations may be completely unrealistic, so that we cannot possibly fit their agenda.

A patient of mind recalled how upset her mother was at her

because the patient, when she was a young girl, did not have blond hair. How tragic.

Childhood wounds caused by a parent's unreasonable expectations can be difficult to heal. One must realize that the parent was wrong and delusional, and this realization cannot be merely of the head or intellect. The heart and the gut must recognize this as well.

Gently ask yourself these questions, and without judgment or criticism observe what thoughts, feelings, and images come into your awareness.

How were your parents unreasonable in their demands and expectations of you? Were you sometimes a pawn in their distorted agendas? Did they live vicariously through you? Did they use you to impress others, such as their friends, siblings, or parents?

An overconcern with the opinions of others is one sign that you were used for such purposes. Ideally it should not matter so much what other people think about you, if you are doing the right thing, seeking your own truth, with compassionate action. Cast off this dependency and be free.

Guilt is a form of self-anger, of anger turned inward. Somehow you disappointed *yourself;* you did not live up to the expectations of your idealized self.

Anger is a defense of the ego, defense against fear. Fear of being humiliated or embarrassed, fear of being minimized, of being mocked, fear of loss and of losing face, indeed fear of losing. Fear of not getting your way. We think anger "protects" us against the others, who would do these things to us, who likewise are angry at us.

Anger is a pernicious and useless emotion. It is dissolved by understanding and by love.

When a negative emotion is understood, when its roots are illuminated, the energy behind the emotion diminishes and even disappears. When you feel angry, the healthy response is to learn what caused the anger, to rectify the situation if that is possible, and then to let go of the anger.

We are all connected. We are all the same. We are all rowing the same boat.

There is often a sadness underneath our anger, as if anger were a protective coating for our vulnerability and despair. Have you noticed how people in love are far less angry? They appear to be in a different rhythm altogether, and anger is not of this rhythm. Nor is sadness of this rhythm. The rhythm of love is of a different sort, and the energies of anger and despair do not resonate with it.

When we are angry we create damaging chemicals in our body that adversely affect our stomach lining, our blood pressure, the blood vessels of the heart and head, our endocrine glands, our immune system, and so on. In addition, anger only gets in the way of effective action. If we could discern the cause of our anger and remedy the causal situation, we would be much better off.

But we still persist in holding onto the anger despite the physical and emotional consequences. We are a stubborn species.

Our media projects angry people as role models for us. Rambo was constantly angry. I don't know if he ever even smiled. Dirty Harry, and seemingly the overwhelming majority of police, soldiers, and other action heroes, are mired in anger. Even Captain Kirk from *Star Trek* was terminally angry.

Their anger is usually portrayed as righteous anger. Somehow they have been wronged, and then it is acceptable to be furious, even to kill.

This portrayal is a great disservice to us. Anger should be eschewed, not encouraged.

Anger encourages us to project our fears onto the "other." Anger causes violence, wars, and incredible heartache. Anger destroys us, from the inside out and from the outside in as well, whether from our own chemical and hormonal secretions or from the bullet of an enemy.

Understanding and love dissolve anger.

I have noticed that if someone cuts me off on the road when I am driving in Miami, where I live, I get angry. When I am on vacation on a Caribbean island and someone does the same thing, I don't get angry. My perspective shifts on vacation, and I don't take rudeness so personally. But anger is not geographical; the shift has occurred within me. It could even happen in Miami.

Letting Go of Fear and Opening Your Mind

You have a relationship with yourself as well as with others. And you have lived in many bodies and in many times. So ask your present self why it is so fearful. Why are you afraid to take reasonable risks? Are you afraid of your reputation, afraid of what others think? These fears are conditioned from childhood or before.

Ask yourself these questions: What's to lose? What is the worst that can happen? Am I content to live the rest of my life this way? Against a background of death, is this so risky?

The walls that we put around ourselves whenever we feel emotionally threatened are walls of fear. We fear being hurt, rejected, ostracized. We are threatened by our vulnerability, and we wall ourselves off so that we do not feel. Our emotions are suppressed.

Sometimes we even reject the person or people who threaten us before they can reject us. We beat them to the punch. This form of self-protection is known as a counterphobic defense. Unfortunately, our walls hurt us more than any other person could. Our walls block us off, close our hearts, worsen our condition. When we are walled off, when we are separated from our emotions and feelings, we can never reach the source of our suffering, the underlying fears and vulnerabilities. We cannot understand the real roots of our problems. We cannot heal; we cannot be whole.

> *Experience transcends belief. Teach them to experience. Remove their fear. Teach them to love and to help one another.*

Close your eyes and take a few deep breaths. Let your walls tumble down. Examine without any judgment, criticism, or guilt what underlies the wall. What is the fear? From what are you protecting yourself? What can you do to heal this fear? How can you become whole again?

Once you truly understand your fear and its sources, the fear will dissolve. Your heart will once again open. You will feel joy.

In a large group regression, Mike had experienced his very first past-life memory. In that life he had been a religious leader, very learned, and he found himself giving a discourse on the masculine and feminine aspects of God. Afterwards, Mike wanted to find out more about this previous life and to discover whether he could remember more about his religious knowledge. This time we were working individually, just the two of us, and the session was taped.

As I have written in previous books, the subconscious mind seems to have its own agenda, its own will. Often it will not respond to my suggestions or even the patient's desires. It will go where it needs to go, not always necessarily where we want it to go.

And so, in a deep trance, Mike found himself in a different

lifetime, in England many centuries ago. He was returning from a war. Apparently there were lessons he needed to learn from this ancient lifetime, lessons that were perhaps more important than the more intellectual content of the life as the religious scholar.

"I'm standing on the outside of a rock wall that runs all the way down to the field. There's a big tree on the other side of the rock wall . . . and I've just come home from, I guess . . . a war . . . because I'm happy to be there, happy to see the land again, and my friend."

Mike continued. "My friend is standing on the other side of the wall. We used to go to the tree, sit by the tree and talk about life and what we were going to do when we grew up and how to deal with what was going on around us. He's waiting for me."

"Can you see him?" I asked.

"He's got brown hair . . . high cheekbones. Well, actually he's got a thin face, not necessarily high cheekbones, but you can see his cheekbones."

I am so frequently impressed by the degree of detail and clarity observed during regressions. Mike continued to describe his friend.

"And sort of a slender build, but not skinny, and he's got . . . like, tight-fitting clothing and he's got a bow and arrows."

"What is the bow for?" I inquired.

"Well, for hunting . . . I mean deer . . . and I guess for protection, too, because I just came back from the war."

"Which war?" I asked.

"A war where we used bows. I have a bow with me also. I also have a rope with two rocks on either end, a thing you throw, my weapons."

"And how do you feel about coming home from this war?"

"I feel great!" Mike immediately responded. "Because I didn't . . . because I'm alive, and now I get to go and be happy again with my friends. I have a father and a mother. I may have a sister; I'm not sure."

I moved him ahead in time, to find out what happened to this young man so happy to be returning home from war.

"I live in a castle on the hill, and it's . . . it's deserted. They took the land while we were gone. My mother's dead, my father is a captive somewhere."

"What happens to you? What do you do now?" I asked.

"I'm just so tired of fighting. I guess I have to do what I'm supposed to do. I guess they depend on me to come back and help them."

I moved him far ahead in time, to the end of that life.

"There's a celebration, that everything is the way it was supposed to be when I came home. And now everybody's happy because we're all happy together, everybody has what they were supposed to have, and the government is back intact. Everything was restored, and I'm reunited with my father and with my friend. My friend and I are going back to sit on the hill."

His life ended in this contented fashion. As he floated above his body after his death in that lifetime, I asked him if there were lessons he learned from that life.

He answered in a peaceful, dreamy tone.

"It's about honor. It's about doing what your purpose is and not being afraid and . . . and believing that everything will work out if you just do what you feel in your heart, and then how important friendship is."

This knowledge was important to Mike, and it is important for all of us. Follow your heart and do not be afraid. Fear blocks us from understanding and following our destiny. Although everything does not always seem to work out on the overt, physical level, these things *always* work out on the spiritual level and even eventually on the physical—if not in this lifetime, then in the next.

⋆   ⋆   ⋆

If your mind is closed, you cannot learn anything new. Closed minds reject anything different, anything that conflicts with their old beliefs, beliefs that may be false. They have forgotten that experience is stronger than belief. Fear is the force that keeps minds closed. Only open minds can receive and process new knowledge.

My mind had been very closed prior to my experiences with Catherine, so I know how difficult it can be to allow one's mind to open to new possibilities. I have asked Carole to write the following account in order to illustrate how my closed mind blocked an important avenue of understanding between us.

From Carole:

We were married slightly less than two years when we received the phone call that my father had died of a sudden, massive heart attack. We hurriedly packed and drove the two hundred miles from our apartment in Connecticut to my parents' home in Pennsylvania. Although my father had a history of heart disease, he was only fifty-three years old, and none of us had expected his death.

My father was a gregarious, charismatic person, and the house was filled with his friends and business associates for the week of mourning.

After the funeral, Brian returned to medical school, and I stayed with my mother for a week or so. My parents had a small, charming Cape Cod house. There were two phones in the house. One was downstairs in a hallway off my parents' bedroom; the other was in the upstairs bedroom I used, on a table a distance away from the foot of the bed. A few days after Brian left I was awakened by the loud ring of the phone in my bedroom. I quickly answered it and heard the unmistakable deep bass voice of my father. He said, "Hello, how is everyone?" Shocked, I answered, "We're very sad, Daddy, because you died, but I think we're going to be all right."

He then asked what my mother had decided to do about his business. My father had owned a scrap-metal business, a junk-yard. My mother had nothing to do with running the business. In fact, she rarely even went there. However, in her grief she could not part with anything of her darling Benjy's, and she decided to try to keep the business going. I told my father this and added that several of his friends (who had similar businesses) were going to help her with advice. He said to tell her to do what she wanted to do; he didn't need her to keep the business.

And then he added, "Tell them that I love them, and I'm okay. You'll never hear from me again."

I hung up the phone with tears streaming down my face. I was wide awake, and although this was a strange occurrence I *knew* that I had actually talked to my father. I was comforted by hearing his voice, but sad that I would never hear from him again.

The next morning I asked my mother and sister if they had heard the phone ring. Neither had heard anything unusual so I was reluctant to tell them of my experience. My mother then said that while she was sleeping she felt someone write "I love you" on the back of her hand. When my parents were in public at a dinner or a movie or a similar place, my father often surreptitiously wrote these words on my mother's hand. She *knew* that he had visited her that night. It was then that I gave them his message.

I returned to Connecticut a few days later. Although the memory of that phone call still haunted me, I didn't tell Brian about it. Anything that hinted at the paranormal was anathema to him. What had happened was so important to me that I didn't think I could stand his rational explanations. This became the only secret in our relationship.

It wasn't until years later, soon after Brian's experience with Catherine, that I told him what I had experienced that night. By that time, he had accumulated a vast library of books relating to such subjects. After listening intently to me, he turned his chair around, reached for a book, and showed me the title: *Phone Calls from the Dead.*

In November of 1992 I read that the Church had finally exonerated Galileo of his "accursed heresy" that the earth was not the center of the solar system. The investigation into Galileo that led to his exoneration had been going on for twelve and a half years.

I was somewhat surprised, because I had assumed that Galileo was cleared in 1722, when Sir Isaac Newton had proved Galileo was correct. But no, here Galileo was, still on the hook, three hundred and sixty years after his discovery. How long it can take to open minds.

A friend pointed out that Galileo died approximately a year before Newton was born. I said, "How interesting. What if Galileo had reincarnated as Sir Isaac Newton and then proved himself correct? He would have been strongly motivated to do so."

My friend added, "And what if he now came back as the pope and cleared himself!"

> You must eradicate the fears from their minds. It is a waste
> of energy when fear is present. It stifles them from fulfilling
> what they were sent here to fulfill. . . . It's only on the sur-
> face . . . that the troubles lie. Deep within their soul, where
> the ideas are created, that is where you must reach them.

During a coffee break at a workshop I was teaching in South America, a woman passed me a note. The note is about overcoming fear, and I'd like to share it with you:

"I've always 'known' and 'seen' that I would die at forty-two. A friend with whom I shared this recommended your book *Many Lives, Many Masters,* because I was becoming very afraid, the closer I got to age forty-two, of my 'vivid' experience of this death.

"While reading the book, I had to put it down because I kept visualizing my 'dream,' plus others that also tormented me. The more I read, the more answers I got. Every time a paragraph made sense, I felt lighter until I came to realize that my tormenting dreams were past-life memories.

"When I saw my friend after reading your book, her first comment was that I looked like I had taken a very heavy load off my shoulders.

"Today I'm two months short of forty-five and carry a much lighter load. Thank you."

A woman told me about a remarkable and vivid NDE she had had several years prior. Sometime after that, she was invited to be a guest on a local television program that was doing a special on NDEs. On the show, she described in detail her own very personal and emotional experience.

Another guest, a psychiatrist who was a skeptical "expert" invited to provide balance on the panel, told her in authoritarian tones that her experience was neither real nor valid, only a chemical reaction in her brain.

"How arrogant of him," I angrily commented when she told me this story. "He knows nothing about the rich visual imagery you encountered, nothing about how emotionally moved you were, nothing about the importance of the messages you received. Yet he dismisses the whole experience as a chemical reaction!"

"No," she softly corrected me. "He was afraid. It was fear, not arrogance."

Of course she was right. Arrogance is merely another face of fear. Without fear, there would be no need for arrogance.

This was an important lesson for me, and I understood. I let my judgmental attitude evaporate in the light of understanding.

Forgiving does not mean forgetting. It means understanding.

Letting Go of Insecurity

"Remember," the voice said. "Remember that you are always loved. You are always protected, and you are never alone. . . . You also are a being of light, of wisdom, of love . . . you can never be forgotten. You can never be overlooked or ignored. You are not your body; you are not your brain, not even your mind. You are spirit. All you have to do is to reawaken to the memory, to remember. Spirit has no limits, not the limit of the physical body nor of the reaches of the intellect or the mind."

One of our greatest faults is our overwhelming concern about outcomes. We are preoccupied with results, and this preoccupation creates unnecessary anxiety, fear, and unhappiness.

The anxiety is about our performance. What if our performance does not measure up? What if we fail? What will the others think? How harshly will we judge ourselves?

The fear relates to the loss of the desired goal or object. If we fail, we are convinced we will not get what we want. We will be failures, losers. We will be rejected. We will hate ourselves.

Instead of worrying about specific outcomes and results, just do the right thing. Reach out unselfishly. Hope for the best.

Hope is fine. Expectation is not, because when expectation is present, disappointment is always lurking nearby.

While meditating one morning, a very clear and distinct message appeared suddenly and powerfully in my mind: "Love one another with all of your hearts and do not fear, do not hold back. For the more you give, the more returns to you."

You yearn for the illusion of security instead of the security of wisdom and love.

Money is neutral, neither good nor bad. What we do with money is the important part. With money we can buy food and clothing for the poor, or we can choose to use it selfishly, squandering the opportunity. The choice is ours, and the lessons will all eventually be learned.

Money and security are not the same thing. Security can only come from within. It is a spiritual trait, not an earthly one. Money is of the earth. You cannot take it with you when you leave.

We can lose everything overnight, if that is our lesson or our destiny. Security derives from inner peace and a knowledge of our true essence, which is spirit. We can never really be harmed, because we are immortal and eternal, because we are spiritual beings, not physical bodies. Because we are always loved and protected. Because we are never alone. Because God and an army of loving spirits always protect us. Because we are all of the same essence. And so there is no need to fear. Indeed, this truth is the secret of our security and our joy.

"Love one another with all of your hearts and do not fear, do not hold back. For the more you give, the more returns to you."

Tom's regression to England in the nineteenth century was very detailed. Even as he described himself, his house, and his circumstances slowly and completely, I knew that he was aware of much more than he was able to verbalize.

In his current life, he was plagued by an unreasonable fear of loss.

In his past life in England, too, he had detected an insecurity. He described a lush country with rolling hills and large old trees. "I'm a landowner . . . mid-forties . . . but I'm not upper-class. . . . My house is like a country estate house. I have a wife and two boys. . . ."

"What has pulled you to this time?" I asked.

"I'm well-to-do; I'm comfortable. I'm sort of established," he answered, "and yet there's some anxiety because I'm not in the upper classes and at any point I'm insecure that they could take it all away or I could lose it."

I advanced him in time to the next significant event in that life.

"There's a fire in the barn," he nervously answered. "It's raging, and I'm trying to get the animals out. . . . A couple of horses I can get out, some of them I can't. . . . I think the house is on fire also!"

"What happens?" I asked.

"The boys are away, but I think my wife dies," he mournfully answered.

"How do you feel?" I asked. "You can remember everything now."

"I'm very distraught," he responded.

"Do you know how the fire began?"

"I think somebody set it." He paused for some moments.

"Do you know who set the fire?" I broke the silence.

"There were people in the village. . . . I think it's because I was Jewish." Again, a profound silence.

After the fire that killed his wife, he left England and came to America, but his sadness continued and he lived a fairly solitary life.

I took him ahead to the last day of that lifetime.

"I'm in the bed. . . . I'm old, and my two boys are there with their families. . . . It's still a little strange being in a new land, but I'm ready to go." He died and left his body.

"I'm aware of . . . There's still this feeling of having been injured for something I was, not for something I did." He had become aware of how anger and prejudice and hate could lead to terrible harm. But there had been a positive lesson also.

"It's my sons . . . that love . . . that family feeling. . . . This was consolation for me."

Tom, who is not Jewish in his current life, had learned far more than the roots of his insecurities and fear of loss. He had learned that hate and prejudice can lead to incredible violence and pain. He had also learned that love is the consolation for all pain.

It was not Tom's task in that past life to punish, or even to judge, those who had burned his house and killed his wife. Karma, divine law, will take care of that. Tom's task is to understand and to forgive. That is the task of love.

The Security of Your Spiritual House

A message awakened me from my sleep. "You are a carpenter building your spiritual home," I heard. "How many hammers are necessary to build your spiritual house? Are one thousand better than one perfect hammer? It is the quality of the house, not how many hammers the carpenter has."

We spend far too much time trying to accumulate hammers and not enough time building our spiritual home.

Sometimes your biological family is not your real family. Your parents, your siblings, and your other relatives may not understand you. They may not express love and caring to you.

They may reject you and treat you cruelly. You are not obligated to be treated inhumanely. There is no karmic responsibility that is met by being a target for the abusive behavior of others, family or not. To abuse or to harm someone is an act of choice or free will by the abuser. Abuse is *never* deserved.

As you grow older, you may find yourself surrounded by friends and others who genuinely care for you, who provide the security that comes from being loved and treated with dignity and respect. These friends and loved ones become your true family. They may share your spiritual values, too, and you may help each other evolve in a positive way. These people are your spiritual family. If you are rejected by your blood family, your family of origin, then your spiritual family takes you in, nurtures you, and becomes the *important* family for you.

I am not saying to abandon your family of origin or not to keep open good communication and a compassionate heart. But you must not allow yourself to be abused, whether psychologically or physically. You must not rationalize abuse as tolerable merely because its source is your family, your friends, or your religious community.

There is an old saying that says blood is thicker than water. This means that when times are tough and your friends or acquaintances may fail you, you can still usually count on your blood relatives to come through for you. I say that if indeed blood is thicker than water, then spirit is thicker than blood. You can always depend on your spiritual family to be there for you.

CHAPTER SIX

How Understanding Heals

All is love. . . . All is love. With love comes understanding.
With understanding comes patience. And then time stops.
And everything is now.

The deepest parts of our minds are not subject to the usual laws of time. Events that occurred long ago can still affect us with penetrating immediacy. Old wounds influence our moods and behavior as if they were inflicted yesterday, and sometimes their power even increases with time.

Understanding can help to heal these old traumas. Because the deeper mind is not subject to the usual conditions of time and space, events of the past can be rescripted and reframed. Cause and effect are not so inextricably bound. Traumas can be undone, and the damaging effects can be reversed. Profound healing can occur, even at vast distances and even after many years of pain and hurt.

Just as love brings profound healing to our relationships, understanding brings a lessening of fear. Understanding opens the window through which love's breeze gently blows away our doubts and anxieties, refreshing our souls and nurturing our relationships.

Our fears are often of events that have already happened, earlier in this life or even from lifetimes long past. Because we have forgotten, we project these fears into the future. But what we fear is actually finished. All we have to do is remember, to awaken to the past.

A young South American woman wrote to me about her awakening and the healing that resulted:

"I have read all your books, and I was really impressed by the stories of people's past lives and even how it can cure certain phobias. In the last few pages of one of your books [*Through Time Into Healing*] you teach the reader how to do a self-hypnotizing procedure. I want to share with you what I saw and felt. Before anything let me explain that I had to do it five times before I really got into a 'trance.' The thing is that I was very nervous before and I wouldn't let myself concentrate. Well, since I met my boyfriend and we started going out (a year and three months ago) I have been very scared of losing him. It was not normal, though, because even suicide went through my mind. The worst was that he never gave me any reason to even think that, since he showed me so many times how much he loves me. One day I was feeling very bad, and I said to myself that it had to stop!

"Then I remembered how I had recorded on the tape the whole procedure. This time I did it with that exact goal: to find out why I was so scared.

"Immediately I could see myself sitting on this starry road. It was 1679, in France. I was French and my name was Marie-Claire. I was around twenty years old and very pretty, with long black hair. I was wearing brown rags and some sandals: this gave me the idea that I was very poor. I had a baby in my arms, and I was crying non-stop. Then I saw someone else in that scene: I recognized him as my boyfriend in today's life. His name was Pedro; he was from Spain. He was around forty years old, and very tall and skinny. We were together, and the baby was ours. He was also desperately crying. Then two guards came into the scene and pulled him away from me. I saw him reaching out his hand for me and screaming for the guards to let him go.

"That was all I saw, for I got too excited and opened my eyes. . . .

"The incredible thing, though, was what I felt afterwards. I wanted to scream of happiness, to laugh a lot. I felt so free and pure inside! The best thing, though, is that I haven't shed one tear over my boyfriend, and those horrible feelings are gone! Our relationship is also much better . . . and I hope this new treatment gets accepted by *all* pretty soon!"

I hope so too, yet I realize that this is more than a treatment. It is an understanding of how life works and how relationships are ever renewed. It is an understanding of how we never really lose our loved ones. Here these two people are, three hundred years later, alive and healthy in new bodies, beginning to share their lives and love once again.

It is this understanding that heals, and through the understanding, love is eternally renewed and manifested.

The two did not meet again by accident or by coincidence. Destiny delicately dictated the rediscovery of their love. Before they were even born again into their present-day bodies, they had already agreed to meet at a certain time in their lives. They would meet, they would "recognize" each other at some deeper level as soul companions through time, and then they would have to make decisions about the future of their relationship in this incarnation. Would their egos, their logical minds, encultured by family and society, interfere with the awareness of their hearts, an awareness stirred by the reunion with a soulmate? Or would their hearts prevail, overriding the obstacles of the conscious mind?

Certain fears and patterns would resurface, in her case the "irrational" fear of an unwanted and tragic separation, because this trauma had happened before, three hundred years ago in France. Since at first she did not remember that ancient event, although her unconscious soul memory knew it well, she feared it would happen in the present or the future.

One of her karmic tasks was to overcome her fear of separation by understanding that love is an absolute energy, that love never ends, not even with the death of the physical body. We are always reunited with our loved ones, either on this side or the other.

Although her soul knew this, she forgot her past-life connections with her lover when she was born into this life. Her task was to remember the immortality of love, to use this knowledge to overcome her fears.

This knowledge leapt from her heart to her conscious mind when she listened to the tape she had made from my book and remembered that French lifetime. Now she knew at all levels, and she immediately let go of her ancient and present-day fear.

She could love freely. She did not need to hold back, fearing the loss of a love.

This young woman's experience is an excellent example of the fact that before we are born, we help to set up and arrange those learning opportunities in our lives, the destiny points, that will help us to understand, to embrace love and relinquish fear. We are helped by divine, spiritual energies in devising our lesson plans. Some feelings of déjà vu represent the dim remembering of our pre-natal plan as it becomes reality in physical state at the designated time and place during the unfolding of our lives. We remember. It is extremely important to pay serious attention to the coincidences, the synchronicities, and the déjà vu experiences in our lives because they often represent the convergence of our spiritual plan and the *actual* path we are traveling during our lifetime.

When we remember, whether through past-life memories, dreams, déjà vu experiences, coincidences and synchronicities, spontaneously, during spiritual moments or mystical events, or in any other way, we begin to understand.

As we understand, we let go of fears.

As we let go of our fears, the obstacles to love disappear and love flows freely within and between and among us.

I am often asked how you know when a "memory" is real and when it may be imagination or fantasy. Interestingly, on the therapeutic level, it does not seem to matter. People get better; their symptoms disappear. It does not even matter whether the patient or the therapist believes in past lives. However, according to a 1994 *USA Today*/CNN/Gallup Poll, 27 percent of Americans do believe in reincarnation. This figure is probably significantly higher today. Ninety percent believe in Heaven.

At the level of validation, however, it does matter. As clinicians and scientists, we would like to know which recollections are real and how to differentiate actual memories from fantasies.

Sometimes differentiating is easy. Someone exhibiting xenoglossy, the ability to speak a foreign language he or she has never learned, is probably touching upon an actual past life. Or else that person has a tremendous psychic ability. The past-life nature of this ability usually becomes apparent during the regression. A person exhibiting detailed knowledge of a particular historical period he or she never studied is another clue. An odd and anachronistic symptom, such as a present-day fear of guillotines, with a subsequent regression to a late-eighteenth-century lifetime, would be another strong indication.

There are several other characteristics of memories that seem to be real. These memories tend to be more vivid and oftentimes more visual than fantasies. The person is more emotionally involved and finds himself or herself in the scene. The scene unfolds like a movie sequence and usually feels familiar. The past-life panorama echoes themes and problems present in the current life. The mirrored problems or symptoms, which may be physical as well as psychological, usually improve or resolve following the remembrance. In addition, the regression scene is not altered by suggestions from the therapist. The scene has a life of its own. And the details of remembered scenes become more and more clear with repetition.

Another frequently asked question is whether or not past-life memories can be explained as genetic memory. That is, are the memories coming from our genes and chromosomes, the genetic or reproductive material that we inherit from our parents, who in turn inherited genes from *their* parents, and so on, all the way back to our most ancient ancestors?

Although some general memories may indeed be passed on through our genes, I do not believe that most past-life memories are obtained this way. There are several reasons to the contrary:

1. Many of my patients have recalled lifetimes in which they died as children or were childless, never having transferred any genetic material at all. The memories of these childless lifetimes are often quite detailed and vivid.

2. The specificity of the memories can be remarkable. A patient may remember a Middle Ages battlefield scene and find exactly the one soldier he was among ten thousand on the field. The wounds of that particular soldier often correspond to a current-life physical ailment, which typically begins to resolve after the past-life scene is recalled. One would not expect such a high degree of specificity with genetic memories. Even the concepts of the collective un-

conscious or of racial memories do not allow for the re-
markably detailed memories that patients often provide.
The memories evoked are not of broad archetypes or categories but of the tiniest details, often accompanied by
powerful feelings and emotions.

3. Many memories have occurred outside of the physical
body, where there is no genetic material. For example, in
the example cited above (which is from actual patient experience), some of the memory is from after the physical
death, when the person was floating above his body and
surveying the scene beneath him. He observed the body
he had just left, its condition and wounds, as well as the
entire battlefield scene and what was still unfolding as the
battle progressed to its end. During his above-the-body visual survey, he also experienced emotions and thoughts.

Remembering: The Key to Happiness in This Life

*To be in physical state is abnormal. When you are in spir-
itual state, that is natural to you. When we are sent back,
it's like being sent back to something we do not know. It will
take us longer. In the spirit world you have to wait, and
then you are renewed. There is a state of renewal. It's a dimension like the other dimensions.*

*We are all spirits . . . some are in physical state and oth-
ers are in a period of renewal. And others are guardians. But
we all go there. We have been guardians, too.*

To remember that we are souls, that we are immortal and always exist in a vast sea of energy, is the key to joy and happiness. In this energetic sea, a host of helping spirits nudge us

along our destiny's pathway, our evolutionary journey toward God-consciousness. We are not in competition with any other souls. We have our path, and they have theirs. There is no race, only a cooperative group journey toward the light of awareness. Souls who are more progressed or evolved reach back with love and compassion to help those behind. The last soul to complete its journey is worth no less than the first.

One particular problem in this school we call the earth is that on earth it is so difficult to remember that we are souls and not just physical bodies. We are constantly distracted by the illusions and delusions of this three-dimensional planet. We are taught that money, power, prestige, material possessions, and other tangible accumulations and creature comforts are extremely important and sometimes even the purpose of our lives. We are taught that we must be liked or respected by others in order to be happy. Being alone, we are told, is being miserable.

In truth, we are immortal beings who never die and are never energetically separated from those we love. We have eternal soulmates and soul families. We are forever guided and loved by guardian spirits. We are never alone.

We do not take our "things" with us when we die. We take our deeds and actions, the fruits of our hearts' wisdom.

When we reawaken to the knowledge that we are all spiritual beings, then our values shift and we can finally become happy and peaceful. What is the difference in this life if you are wealthy and I am not? Only the treasures of spirit can be retained. What is the difference if you are powerful or famous and I am not? Happiness has no roots in power or fame, only in love. What is the difference if you are more liked and respected by others than I am? Perhaps I am daring to tell and to live the truth, and the truth is rarely popular. Happiness comes from within, not from without, not from the reflection of what others think of you. Jealousy is poison to the soul.

So our goal is to remember, to reawaken. Perhaps one story or one paragraph in this book might stimulate your memory, stir you to awaken, raise your consciousness. To paraphrase Clint Eastwood's famous movie line, that would "make my day."

Perhaps one reason that more people do not have spontaneous memories of their past lives is because learning in the physical body is a field test. We must ensure that our spiritual gains and knowledge are ingrained in our very essence. If we are non-violent only because the memory of a brutal past lifetime makes us fear future consequences of similar behavior, we have not completely learned our lesson. We have learned our lesson if we practice non-violence because we *know* in our hearts that violence itself is wrong.

I do not believe, however, that we are not meant to have access to these memories. Through hypnosis, recall is much easier, lessons are remembered from a higher perspective, symptoms are relieved, and spiritual understanding can be dramatically accelerated.

Nancy's experience demonstrates this process.

Nancy was casually dressed in beige shorts and a white T-shirt. Everyone in my three-day workshop at Omega Institute, a holistic learning center in Rhinebeck, New York, had spent the weekend in the beautiful Catskill foothills, and we all felt very relaxed. Group regression sessions had added to the tranquil mood.

Along with four others, Nancy had volunteered to be regressed in front of the large group. I chose her because I sensed she could benefit from an individual regression, where I could ask questions and guide the process more specifically. I could not get the individual feedback in large group exercises.

Because she was a volunteer and not a patient, the regression was designed to be a demonstration of technique, not a therapy session. However, once a person enters into this deeply relaxed and yet actively focused state of consciousness, healing often occurs. The subconscious mind doesn't care about my intentions, as long as it is safe and protected. For Nancy, here was a healing opportunity, a learning situation, and such a golden opportunity was not to be missed.

We talked in private for a few moments, and I described the procedure we would be using. I had decided to use a rapid induction technique. With this method I could bring Nancy into a deep hypnotic state in less than twenty seconds.

"Okay, Nancy, just like we talked about, putting your right hand into mine, keep your eyes on my eyes. Then it's just following the directions. Is that okay?"

She quickly agreed.

"Good. In a moment I am going to count to three. When I reach three, press down firmly with your hand. You'll feel my hand pressing up. You should be keeping your eyes on mine and following the directions. One . . . two . . . three. Eyes getting heavy, droopy, drowsy, closing, sleepy. Let them close, closing—*sleep!*"

I quickly pulled my hand from under hers, and she fell immediately into a deep trance. I then brought her even deeper with several deepening techniques, and asked her what she was experiencing.

After a few moments of silence, she began to speak.

"My first Holy Communion. We're in a car and my grandfather is taking us to get ice cream. It's my special day. Everybody's paying attention to me, and I'm really excited." She smiled radiantly.

"And about how old are you?"

"Six," she answered without hesitation.

"Can you see what you're wearing?"

"White dress. I have my white shoes and my white anklets

with lace on the trim. I'm pretty and I'm excited and everybody's telling me how pretty I am."

"And this is a happy time for you?" I asked, even though the answer was obvious.

"Yes."

"Can you see the other people who are there with you?" Visual anchors are always important.

"Yes. My grandfather, my mother, my sister, and my brother."

"How do they look to you?"

"They look . . . we're driving, and we're in a car. They're in the car with me, naturally, in the car, my brother and my sister in the backseat with me. They're younger, they're . . . I don't know how old they are."

"This is a happy memory for you. Is that what you're feeling, happy?" I asked this because I could see some tears forming in the corners of her eyes.

"Yes."

"Those tears that are in your eyes, are they happiness tears or sad ones?"

"I'm excited."

Now that I knew the memory was a happy one, I decided to summarize and to move farther back in time. "That's a wonderful memory, and you know everything that happens after that. A good memory. You're in the white dress looking beautiful; everybody's paying attention to you. I want you to take back with you, even after you're awake, this happy, happy memory with the good feelings and also the feelings of loving yourself, self-love. Because it's not just on one day or one special day; you can love yourself every day. Every day can be that kind of special day for you. Remembering the happy feelings of that time and bringing them into the present time so that you're happy now. You're bringing these happy feelings of the little girl with the white dress and the communion and the family and all the attention and the affection and the love that's there from the family. You'll be able to bring all of that back with you. Is that okay?" She nodded as she soaked in lessons of love.

"Are you ready to go farther backward?" She nodded again.

"Float above now, float above the scene, and let it begin to fade away. You'll bring back all the happy memories and the self-love, but let the scene fade away. Let the scene fade away. Now you're just floating, so free and so peaceful, so calm. Let's go back before you were born, in utero, in your mother's womb. Is that okay?" Again she agreed.

"Let's just see what comes to you from this time, if anything. I'll tap you on the forehead and count backwards again from five to one. Go back, before you were born, in utero, in your mother's womb, and just see if you have any feelings, perceptions, impressions, thoughts, or sensations from this time."

After a few moments, she began.

"I'm floating. I feel love. My mother has back pain. I sense that she presses on her back."

"And you're wanted. You feel the love that's ready to greet you."

"Yes. Lots of stuff going on now. Busy, busy, busy. I guess, getting ready . . . they are . . . getting ready."

"What are they doing?" I inquired.

"They are painting, and they're getting moving people."

"And you're aware of all of this?" I asked, impressed by how many details she had already perceived.

"Yes, but they're excited. It's good activity."

"Why are there tears?" I observed that her tears had reappeared.

"I don't know. I'm happy."

"Another memory for you to bring forward, that of being wanted, the excitement. Because the preparation is normal— painting, getting the room ready, getting ready for you to make your arrival. You're a *wanted* baby; they're looking forward to it. There's a lot of love there. You can feel it as you float, and that's very important. Now let's go through the birth, so that the birth is just finished. As I count to three, be through with it. No pain, no discomfort, and see how you are greeted and how the people felt. What was the reception like? One, two, three. Good. Now you're born and you're fine. What do you become aware of now?"

"It's cold," she answered, and she began to shiver. "My mother is not awake, she's not there. She doesn't know that I'm there. It's just indifference, it's just another baby. The doctors and the nurses are just doing what they have to do." I thought that her mother must have been unconscious because of the general anesthesia. The doctors and nurses were doing their jobs, but Nancy was already aware that they did their work without much emotion.

"Not the love that your mother has for you."

"Yeah, I guess."

"Do they wrap you in something to help you keep warmer?"

"I can't tell."

Her shivering and chills were becoming more severe, so I decided to take her away from the delivery room.

"Now we're going to float above and leave that scene, and you will warm up again. Warm yourself up. Floating above, let the scene fade away and disappear. Now you're warm, you're comfortable, just floating again. Are you ready to go farther back now?"

"Yes."

"Good. So let's just take one more trip, one more stop, and let's go back even farther. If there is any past life for you to remember, you will be able to remember that now, as I tap you on the forehead and count backwards from five to one. Let a scene or an image of a past life come into focus, and pay attention to any details. As I reach one, it will be in complete focus. You'll be able to stay in a deep, deep state continuing to experience and to tell me what you are experiencing, a past-life scene or whatever comes to you, what's important for you. You'll be able to remember as I count to one. Five, you can remember everything. Four, something from a past life. Three, let it come into focus now. Two . . . one. Good. Just be there with it. You can pay attention to clothes or other details, architecture, houses, topography or geography, yourself. Are there other people around? Whatever you become aware of is fine. You'll be able to talk and still stay in a deep state, continuing to experience. You'll be able to tell me what you become aware of, what you experience."

"I'm in a village," she answered, her eyes fluttering under the lids. "It's a center of the town, like a market. There's a lot of activity, lots of people hollering above each other, like an auction. An auction. I'm passing by; I'm not part of this. I'm a man. I have a beard. It smells, there're lots of smells and odors. It's not clean; it's dirty." She continued to scan this scene, taking in many details.

"What does the marketplace look like? How are people dressed? Is it open-air? What kind of things are they selling?" I was trying to get an approximate time period.

"It's open, with tents. It's dry, it's dusty. Chickens and vegetables, but not a lot of vegetables. People—they're like peasants, it's the back streets of something."

"Of a bigger city?"

"I see a wall. There's a wall dividing this area from another area. I want to say Egypt, but it's not Egypt. It was Egypt, it is Egypt." I suspected an area of frequent invasions and conquests, with shifting boundaries.

"And now let's go ahead in time to see what happens to the man. He's passing through, this man with a beard . . . what happens to him? Let's go into the future, to the next significant event in your life . . . this man's life. . . . As I tap on your forehead and count to three, go to the next significant event. One, two, three. Just let it happen. Once again, you'll be able to experience and stay in a deep, deep state and you'll be able to talk and to tell me what you're experiencing, of what you become aware, what's happening to you."

"A meeting. He's meeting with people. He's important. He knows . . . he's telling people things that have happened in other places. Changes, changes . . . I don't know what the changes are. People don't want the changes."

"And how does he feel? How do you feel?" I deliberately included "he" and "you" to intensify her connection to this ancient man.

"He's anxious. He's not sure how they want to receive this."

"But it's important information, the changes need to be made?"

"He knows he has to tell them. He can't not tell them. He was told he has to tell them."

"I'm going to tap you on the forehead and see if you can get any more detail of what he has to tell them, what kind of changes. Three, any details that come to you . . . two . . . one."

"I see a paper. I think it's a map. I can't get . . ." She paused for a moment.

"I sense an army," she continued. "A mass of people are going to be coming. Yes. I think they're taking over this land. I think they're coming in and telling them they have to move on or else they'll be forced off. And if the people don't go, they're going to fight."

"And what is your role in this? Which side are you on? What are you accomplishing?"

"I think I'm on the other side. I'm warning them. I'm almost a spy. They each think I'm helping them but I'm trying to keep peace between them."

"That's a good thing, to avoid war. That's important, but it's dangerous for you."

"I'm scared." I could see the anxiety etched on Nancy's face. I progressed her in time.

"Let's go ahead in time again and see what happens to you. It's a very delicate and dangerous situation. You're scared. An army is coming and you're kind of a forerunner to this, to try to work it out peacefully so there's not a war, because you don't know which way these people are going to go now. But let's go ahead and see what happens. Three . . . two . . . let it all come to you, you can remember everything. One. It's okay to remember. It's okay to remember what happens, what happens to the people and the land."

"I'm in the desert. I'm out of that area. I did what I was supposed to do. They started fighting among themselves. Some wanted to believe me, and some didn't. Once I knew that they got my message I left, and I'm moving on. I don't know where I'm going, it's unknown. I'm just going in the desert, and I'm alone."

"Are you older now?"

"I'm not much older. . . ." She grew silent and we waited. Finally, I broke the silence.

"Let's go ahead now to the end of that life. A spy, scout, advance messenger. Go ahead to the end of your life as I tap you on the forehead again, the very last moments, and see what happens. You can become aware of everything now. Five, you can remember it all . . . four, the very last day . . . three, of this man's life . . . two . . . one. Okay, you're at the very end now. What do you become aware of?"

"I'm in a friend's house. I'm dying. I'm peaceful." Her face reflected this peace.

"Can you see your friend?"

"I feel them. They're very good friends. It's a man and a

wife. They've taken care of me for the last few years. I'm very old."

"So you survived the danger and you lived to an old age. Now it's time to go, so you can float out of that body now, go through it, just dying of old age. Floating above and feeling so free and light now, and peaceful, just floating and reviewing that life in your mind. The lessons . . . what did he learn? What were the lessons of that life, which was a complicated and important but difficult life? Very much living on the edge. What did you learn? What did he learn?" Nancy contemplated the lessons.

"I had to sacrifice. My happiness wasn't always important. I had a bigger chore. I had to leave my family to save others."

"A kind of duty that you had."

"Yes, it was worth it. It was good. I'm satisfied."

"It helped to bring peace, or at least to avoid war in many circumstances," I added.

"Yes, I think I did. I never really know."

"Because you go on to the next place?"

"Yes, I move and I don't always hear back from that area again."

"Very good. In your mind, make the connections to your life now, as Nancy. What can you bring from that life, with the discipline, the authority, the compassion, the sense of duty that he had, to your life? See the connections and what you can learn from this . . . his strength. Just bring it into your own life now. You don't have to talk and tell me. This is for you privately. Bring this into Nancy's life, all of these qualities that you need or can bring forward, that you've had before. See the connections. Bring it into Nancy's life, and into your life now."

We waited. I sensed when she had accomplished the task I had set before her. "Good. Are you ready to come back now?"

"Yes."

"Okay. I'm going to awaken you in a few moments by pressing upwards on a point between your eyebrows on your forehead. When I press upwards, then you can open your eyes. You'll be awake and alert, all the way back, right here, remembering everything, and in complete control of your body and your mind." I pressed upwards, and she slowly opened her eyes, looking dazed. She had returned from a very deep state, a very long journey.

"Good. Welcome back. How did that feel to you? What was that experience like?"

"I felt like I was watching something that I wasn't experiencing, although I *was* experiencing it. It was very different."

"And kind of intense, too," I added.

"Very intense," she agreed. "I knew an importance was there, but I didn't understand the importance of things at the time, until after I looked back and then I realized that everything worked the way it was supposed to."

"Good. On the way you had a good memory of childhood, the communion. Remember the white dress and that special feeling you had? You had siblings so you didn't get that often."

"Number five of seven," she clarified. "So you didn't always have attention paid to you."

"Right. That was your day, though."

"Right. I was queen for the day," she answered proudly, remembering her communion.

"Then we went back to your birth time, in utero and being born. Again you were aware of love, of being greeted, the preparations that were going on. So you were really wanted. Even though fifth, you were wanted, and that's important. Your parents were excited about you. And you felt the difference in the energy between the doctors and nurses who were just doing their jobs, and your parents where there was love and waiting for you and getting ready for you and all the preparations."

"I felt very distant at that time, that they were not as connected to me or as excited about me being there." She was talking about the medical staff. "It was another birth, and they had to take care of the mechanics."

"Then the memory of the man with the beard in the desert. Maybe Egypt or Asia Minor, that area."

She had a faraway look in her eyes as she remembered even more. "I saw him walking down a road, with rolling hills, a long dirt road with fields on either side. He was alone."

"He was paving the way so that the armies wouldn't have to lose soldiers unnecessarily. Trying to get them just to acquiesce rather than to fight," I observed.

Nancy knew more. "I really sense that even though he lived his life solitarily, he wasn't alone, he never felt alone. Something connected him to this purpose, I think."

"And I wanted you to see the connections to you now, but not to talk about it, because that's personal stuff. Do you mind if people ask you a question or two?" She agreed. The audience had been spellbound and it took a few moments before anyone ventured a question.

"When did this take place?"

Nancy thought for a moment before answering. "From what I could sense of the dress, I don't know the time but I feel a sense of B.C., but I don't know when. I didn't have a sense of the year."

As Nancy answered this question, my mind began to wander back to Catherine, my first regression patient, about whom *Many Lives, Many Masters* was written. Catherine had also mentioned a date as B.C. For years critics have jumped on this as some sort of fatal contradiction. "How could she know B.C. when the term 'B.C.' was not a concept in that ancient time?" they would exult. And here was Nancy, doing the same thing.

Of course, the answer is simple when you understand the

process of hypnosis and age regression. In hypnosis, the person is the observer as well as the person being observed. In fact, many people in trance state watch the past as if they are observing a movie. Your conscious mind is always aware of and observing what you are experiencing while you are hypnotized. Despite the deep subconscious contact, your mind can comment, criticize, and censor. This is why people who may be hypnotized and actively involved in a childhood or past-life sequence of memories are able to answer the therapist's questions, speak their current-life language, know the geographical places they are seeing, and even know the year, which often flashes before their inner eyes or just appears in their minds. The hypnotized mind, *always retaining an awareness and knowledge of the present,* puts the childhood or past-life memories into context. For example, if the year 1900 flashes, and you find yourself in ancient garb building a pyramid in ancient Egypt, you *know* that the year is B.C., even if you don't see those actual letters.

People can remember events from the earliest days of their infancy, as we have seen, and yet still speak perfect English. Why? Because they are remembering. They don't actually become infants again and lose all of their physical and mental abilities.

My attention was jolted back to Nancy and the audience. Another question was being asked.

"Does Nancy have any feeling as to why she particularly chose that life, as opposed to any other life, to experience now? Or did it just come to you?"

Nancy answered. "I have no idea why that one came. I think in the last section, to talk about what I need to be doing in my life now, I think that's probably a valuable lesson I need to know and I need to contemplate. So maybe that's what I really need to hear and understand, about the solitude, I think."

After a few more questions on technique, I ended the session. A few days later Nancy wrote to me:

"Your work is making a difference in many people's lives. I personally have experienced an empowering growth since reading . . . your books. I haven't even begun to absorb the experience of this weekend, although I understand the message I received and see its importance in this lifetime. I know it will have a dramatic impact on my life and the lives of those around me.

"Thank you for the freedom you have given me to experience and acknowledge my own eternal soul!"

Nancy had captured the essence of her sacred journey.

Feeling Joy and Happiness Every Day: Lessons for the Heart

Never lose the courage to take risks. You are immortal. You can never be hurt.

Sometimes the lessons learned seem simple or obvious, yet they must be learned by our hearts, at the deepest levels, not only by our intellects. Direct experience, often through regressions, can provide an avenue to the heart.

Barbara was going through a detailed and deeply felt past life in the American South during the second half of the nineteenth century.

She remembered the large white house where she lived with her mother in the aftermath of the American Civil War and the hardship they endured there. She remembered a happier time from later in that life when she was married, with two young children, and living in a different house. I moved her to the last day of that lifetime.

"I'm old . . . my hands have spots on them . . . brown spots on my hands, and the skin is very soft."

"Is there anyone around?" I asked.

"My son is with me . . . my daughter is there . . . she's by the doorway, she's looking at me. She's *sad*," Barbara lamented in a whisper. "I don't want her to be sad."

She died, floating above the old body she left behind.

"How do you feel now?" I inquired.

"Better," she answered in a stronger voice. "I can see them in the room. I can see the woman in the bed," she added, observing her former body. "She has white hair, and she's wrinkly. . . . I feel very peaceful. . . . I feel like I'm floating . . . floating."

She was enjoying this peaceful place. Before awakening her, I asked her to take a long look at her daughter and her son, to see if she recognized them as anyone in her present life as Barbara.

"I got a sense that the daughter is a niece that I have now by the name of Rebecca . . . it was weird. . . . I feel the connection that that daughter is now her."

I reminded Barbara that we often come around again and again with the same people, even though our relationships may change. This is one way we learn here in the physical state.

After floating above her withered old body, she was able to review that lifetime, its affluent beginnings, the devastation after the Civil War, and the happy family life that followed. One lesson stood out above the others.

"To slow down and to appreciate what you have around you," Barbara said emphatically.

Once again, although the lesson applies specifically to her, it also applies to all of us.

There is so much beauty, so much truth and love around us, but we so rarely slow down enough to notice, to appreciate. Sometimes it takes a tragedy or a great loss to remind us, but quickly we seem to fall back into the same old rut.

"Slow down and smell the flowers" is the modern version of Barbara's lesson. Enjoy the fruits of this beautiful garden. It is not enough that your intellect, your head, understands this. Your heart must, also, and your daily thoughts and actions must show that your heart truly knows.

Sit or lie comfortably and close your eyes. Take a few relaxing breaths and let all the tightness and discomfort leave your body.

Remember those times when your eyes misted with tears of happiness and joy. Perhaps you unselfishly helped another human being. Perhaps somebody, unasked and unexpectedly, reached out to help you. Perhaps you were reading a book or watching a movie or witnessing a scene where lives were being touched by love.

Take your time. Your heart is opening.

Whenever your eyes well up with tears of joy, carefully stop and observe. What are you witnessing? Why does this touch you? What is missing in your life?

Now you have a strong clue about which modifications are needed to bring more joy, more happiness, more peace into your life.

It is well known that happiness comes from within. Happiness is an inner state. You will not miraculously become happy if someone else changes, or if the outside world changes, but only if *you* change. You must see with a larger perspective. Someone else may point the way, give you techniques, but that is all others can do. The rest is up to you.

It is not wrong, sinful, or unspiritual to be happy and to

have fun. You cannot graduate from this school until you learn to be joyful.

Mother Teresa wrote, "I am sure that if we all understand the Golden Rule—that God is Love and that He has created us for greater things, to love and to be loved—we would then love one another as He has loved each one of us. True love is a giving until it hurts. It is not how much we give—but how much love we put into the giving.

"Therefore it is necessary to pray—the fruit of prayer is deepening of Faith—the fruit of Faith is Love—Love in action is Service—and so acts of Love are acts of Peace—and this is the living of the Golden Rule.

"Love one another as God loves each one of us."

I do not agree that true love is a giving until it hurts, because there is too much joy in such giving. Any hurt would be quickly soothed. But the rest is pure wisdom. If everyone were to follow Mother Teresa's simple prescription, violence and war would disappear, and peace would reign over the world.

At an inner, psychological level, people would feel this peace also. Fears would diminish and disappear, since love dissolves fear. Without fear, we could accomplish what we came here to accomplish. We would also be happier. The walls we hide behind would evaporate because we would not need to insulate ourselves emotionally if we did not fear. We could open ourselves to the energy of love.

I once treated a professional golfer who was overly concerned with his scores. The more anxious he became, the more strokes he lost on the course.

During a particularly deep meditation in my office, he left his ego behind and "merged" with the golf course. He began to understand golf as a metaphor for life. The course throbbed with life; it became animate.

"What did you learn?" I asked him.

"That the course doesn't care what I score or how I play. It only wants me to enjoy it, to feel its beauty and its gifts. Its greatest wish is to provide pleasure and joy."

This man has made remarkable spiritual progress. Not surprisingly, when he gives golf lessons he gives lessons about life also. His students are doubly benefited—and his scores have dropped significantly.

While I was meditating one day, a message came in answer to an unasked question that had been forming in my mind. I was working hard, at the office treating patients, with lectures and conferences, with a mountain of correspondence. What about vacations, reading for pleasure, playing golf without keeping score (my variation on the game)? Should I take more time for myself and my family and my friends? Enjoy the simple pleasures of life more? Or is the work too important?

The message was emphatic in tone:

"This world is given to you as a beautiful garden. You diminish the garden if you do not enjoy its fruits."

Awareness

You should check your vices before you come to this point. If you do not, you carry them over with you to another life. Only we can rid ourselves . . . of the bad habits that we accumulate when we are in a physical state. The Masters cannot do that for us. If you choose to fight and not to rid yourself, then you will carry them over into another life. And only when you decide that you are strong enough to master the external problems, then you will no longer have them in your next life.

The Jesuit priest and psychologist Tony de Mello tells a story about awakening, about becoming aware that we are asleep in our everyday ruts.

A father becomes aware that his son is oversleeping again and will be late for school. He raps repeatedly on his son's door.

"Wake up, wake up, you'll be late for school!" the father says loudly.

"I don't want to go to school," his son answers.

"Why not?" asks the father.

"Three reasons," responds the son. "First, because school is so boring; second, the kids tease me all the time; and third, I *hate* school!"

"I am going to give you three reasons why you *must* go to school," the father retorts. "First, because it is your duty; second, because you are forty-five years old; and third, because you are the headmaster!"

So wake up and climb out of your rut. If you stay asleep, you will grow old still asleep and you will miss your life's potential.

Live in the present, not the past or the future. The past is over; learn from it and let it go. The future is not yet here. Plan for it, but do not worry. Worry only wastes your time and energy.

The Vietnamese Buddhist monk Thich Nhat Hanh describes enjoying a good cup of tea. You must be in the present moment, mindful and aware, to enjoy the tea, to savor the sweet aroma, to taste the flavor, to feel the warmth of the cup. If you are ruminating about past events or worrying about future ones, you will look down at your cup and the tea will be gone. You drank it, but you do not remember, because you were not aware.

Life is like that cup of tea.

> *When you are not experiencing the present, when you are*
> *absorbed in the past or worried about the future, you bring*
> *great heartache and grief to yourself.*

A doorway to an expanded awareness may open during the regression experience. If the therapist is ready and flexible, allowing the other person's higher mind to guide the process gently rather than pursuing the therapist's own agenda, a life-transforming experience may occur. Such was the case with John.

As I hypnotized John, a middle-aged and well-educated man, before an audience of several hundred people in a Boston workshop, an awareness that the audience had grown unusually quiet, hanging expectantly on every word, seeped into my consciousness.

Gently and gradually, I nudged him back in time. His first image was of a Christmas party when he was five years old. He beamed with childlike pride as he vividly remembered the scene.

"My aunts are there. I can see them. I'm wearing my first suit . . . gray flannel!" He felt very grown-up to be wearing that suit. "I see the tree, filled with lights," he continued.

I was silent for a while, letting him enjoy this long-ago event, experiencing his pride and his happiness.

Then I led him farther back, back before he was born, back to the in-utero environment, in his mother's womb.

Immediately he said, "It's so tight in here! I want to stretch."

John began to move his head around, stretching his legs, carefully moving his arms. Then he noticed a "sparkling light" rippling through the umbilical cord, and the light relaxed him.

I took him through his birth, and although he experienced no physical discomfort, he was bothered by all the noise.

"So many people are talking," John explained.

I instructed him to detach from the scene of his birth, still remaining in a deep hypnotic state. I then asked him to visualize and walk through a special door, expecting him to recover a past-life memory, but he did not. His experience was a spiritual one instead.

John found himself in a beautiful garden. He described a wondrous, diffuse light that filled the garden, a light that infused him with a sense of profound peace. He became aware of children, many children. He related that he was older and a teacher to the children.

As he observed a white horse nearby, the word *purity* flashed into his mind. A solitary shade tree stood on his right. John spoke very slowly and deliberately. Words could not adequately describe the scene unfolding before him. Words could not describe the qualities of the light or of the garden. I could sense that he knew far more than he could share with the rest of us.

"What do you teach the children?" I asked.

His answer was enigmatic at first. "I teach them how to play," he answered slowly and softly. Then his voice became much firmer, as if we in the audience had become the children, and he was now a teacher to us.

"We can be there always!" he said. "We can be there always."

John's voice trailed off and he was silent. And then he began to speak very quietly, whispering as if he wanted me to hear, even more so than the others.

"This joy . . . beauty . . . awareness, this garden on earth could be there all the time, whenever we choose. It can be there now, in the present, if we chose . . . if we remembered how." He was silent again as tears of joy quietly rolled down his cheeks. John did not want to leave that place, so I let him rest there.

And this is what John taught the children: Paradise on earth is possible if we choose it. John's message is very powerful. We can become conscious of the "other" reality now, even in our present state, even in physical form. We can feel the pure joy, the ecstasy, the peace, and the beauty even now. And when we pass beyond the physical state, we become aware of the same, we go to the same, we really *are* the same. Our forgetfulness, our state of being "unconscious," is reversible. We do not need to die, or have an NDE, to remember, to reexperience. Tears of joy continued to flow from John's eyes.

He realized, as did I, that a shift was happening in his life, a shift from the overly intellectual into the experiential. An opening had occurred and would not close, because the experience was so positive and so powerful.

John wrote to me two weeks later, describing synchronous events that affirmed his experience even more. Symbols of gardens were appearing everywhere. He walked into a music store and felt immediately "guided" to a CD called *Secret Garden.* He read the description: "14 new Celtic and Norwegian melodies to help you discover your own secret garden."

Then when John walked into a bookstore to purchase a particular book, his "awareness was drawn to another book, which was *Beyond the Garden Gate,* with beautiful light-filled paintings of gardens and poems."

Several days later he walked into an elevator, and he found a poem from the first or second century taped to the wall:

> All Those Who Love You
>   are beautiful
> They overflow with your presence
> They can do nothing but good.
>
> There is space in your garden
> All of us are welcome there
> All we need to do is enter.

John added, "Everywhere I turn gardens continue to come into my awareness. . . . Reaching the garden through the heart and being in touch with the garden of the soul."

During John's experience in Boston, my awareness had also begun to shift.

"It can be there now, in the present, if we choose," he had said. We do not have to forget. We can maintain our awareness that we are divine beings who can *directly* experience joy, love, infinite compassion, profound feelings of safety and peace—all right now.

Just by witnessing, watching, and sharing, an opening in the awareness of several hundred people in the audience in Boston was also occurring. Feelings of joy, of peace, of safety were everywhere in the room, as if a vapor of higher truth was filling us with the messages that we are immortal, and we are always loved. We *are* love. Love is the energy that fills every atom of our being, and there is nothing to fear.

✈ Chapter Seven ✞

Love and Compassion

Love is the ultimate answer. Love is not an abstraction but an actual energy, or spectrum of energies, which you can "create" and maintain in your being. Just be loving. You are beginning to touch God within yourself. Feel loving. Express your love.

Love dissolves fear. You cannot be afraid when you are feeling love. Since everything is energy, and love encompasses all energies, all is love.

The majority of us do not live our lives as if we were aware of our spiritual nature. We act as if we are just physical objects, with neither souls nor spirit. Otherwise we would never do the insane things we keep doing. More than 90 percent of us believe that there is a God, that heaven exists, and that we go to another realm when we die. But our behavior belies these beliefs. We treat each other rudely and violently. We still commit genocidal acts and fight incessant wars. We murder and rape, we torture and steal. We continue to behave in very crude and selfish ways.

Fear prevents us from recognizing our true spiritual

essence. Spiritual beings such as we are should be practicing compassion and charity, not murder and robbery. We have so many fears.

If you must think in terms of reward and punishment, consider that you will be abundantly rewarded for thoughts and acts of love and compassion. You will be invariably punished for acts of hatred and violence. Still, we don't seem to understand this; instead, oftentimes we find the expression of love more frightening. We fear being rejected, being ridiculed, being humiliated, being perceived as "weak," being labeled, or being foolish.

Yet even these fears are false: We are always loved and always protected. We are spiritual beings in a vast spiritual sea, populated by innumerable other spiritual beings. Some are in physical form, but most are not.

Love is the water of this sea.

Love is an energy, the highest and most pure energy. At its highest vibrations love possesses both wisdom and awareness. It is the energy that unites all beings. Love is an absolute and it never ends.

When physicists in their laboratories measure the energies that healers emit, whether they direct this energy toward patients, bacterial cultures, or elsewhere, I believe these energies are related to the energy of love (spiritual energy). Healing energy is a component of spiritual energy. With future research and improved technology, we will better understand this connection.

When physicians talk about the mind-body connection, I believe love is the connecting energy.

When religions talk about the nature of God, love is always mentioned. This is true for all religions and unites all of us.

One characteristic of energy is its vibratory pattern. Gas molecules vibrate more rapidly than molecules of liquids, which in turn vibrate more rapidly than molecules of solids.

The molecules may be identical, such as H_2O (water), but the frequency of molecular vibration determines the state, whether solid or liquid or gas.

It is not far-fetched to imagine that there is only one pure energy, that which we call love. As its vibration is diminished, its state changes. We are the solid form.

Two of our main goals during our lifetime are redemption and inner peace. By redemption I mean freedom. Redemption implies the overcoming of karma, through our actions and through grace. There are many paths to redemption. When we are redeemed, we have reclaimed our soul's destiny.

Redemption here is not meant in the Christian or religious sense, but rather as the process of enlightenment and liberation from the cycle of physical life and death. Redemption is a gradual process, inexorably leading us to our spiritual home. Once liberated, the soul may choose to return to the physical plane in order to help others along the pathway to redemption.

Redemption comes from love, not from suffering. When our hearts overflow with love and our love flows to the others, we are in the process of redemption. We are fulfilling and canceling our karmic debts. We are being drawn back to the bosom of God, who is ultimate love.

Achieving inner peace alone is not enough. The monastic or ascetic experience is a means to an end, not the end itself. Reaching a state of calm while sitting in a cave in Tibet is admirable, but you have only reached first base. To be living in a physical world requires physical actions: to reach out to others in order to relieve their suffering and help them along their path; to be empathetic and compassionate; to help heal the planet, its inhabitants, and its structures; to teach as well as to learn.

If you are engaged in this process, you will gain inner peace—even if you haven't a spare moment to spend in a cave.

Expecting Nothing in Return

The rest of us continue to ask for rewards—rewards and justifications for our behavior . . . when there are no rewards, rewards that we want. The reward is in doing, but doing without expecting anything . . . doing unselfishly.

My wife has taught me a great deal about love. She supports me in the shadows, never seeking the limelight and making sure none of the spotlights, so frequently shining on me, are reflected on her. She works silently and in private, asking for nothing in return. She watches patiently as others take my time and energy, stealing from her, too, because I should be there more for her. She understands.

She sometimes tells me, in a jesting way, that she loves me more than I love her. I always say no, I love her as much.

But I believe she is right. She does love me more. Because even though I love her enormously, she knows more about love than I do. She *knows how* to love more.

I can only promise her that I am learning, and I will catch up.

Compassion

Albert Einstein stated: "A human being is part of the whole we call the universe, a part limited in time and space. He experiences himself, his thoughts and feelings as something separated from the rest—a kind of optical illusion of his consciousness. This illusion is a prison for us, restricting us to our personal desires and to affection for only the few people nearest us. Our task must be to free ourselves from this prison, by widening our circle of compassion, to embrace all living beings and all of nature."

In August of 1996 I visited Brazil for the first time. Spending some time amidst the incredible people and physical wonders of this very spiritual land, I was able to get to know Geraldo, my Brazilian book publisher.

As a special preface to *Through Time Into Healing*, which was then being published in Brazil, I wrote the following about Geraldo because he demonstrates the principle of love in action:

"One of my most enduring memories of Brazil is that of a young girl's face. She is about twelve years old, and I can see her shining eyes and hear her throaty laugh as she and a few dozen other young girls darted past me to their 'work stations.'

"I had been brought to a very special place by my publisher, Geraldo Jordão Pereira, a wonderful man. He and his wife, Regina, have been instrumental in starting and sustaining a project for underprivileged young girls in a poor suburb of Rio de Janeiro. The girls come to the center, consisting of a few small buildings, and learn practical skills: sewing, typing, hair and nail care, and so on. They bond together; their self-esteem is enhanced, and they master useful and marketable skills. Their joy and happiness were overflowing as they demonstrated to me what they had mastered.

"I was touched by the energy of that place and those girls. And Geraldo, who brought me there that day, exemplifies to me the spirit of Brazil. Here is an intelligent and sophisticated man who gives so much back, and with so much passion, to the land and the people. . . .

"This is why we are here, on this earth. To learn to reach out to our fellow human beings with love and compassion, without concern for what comes back to us personally. When I saw the girls' exuberant, loving faces, I knew that Geraldo, and Brazil, were succeeding."

I had a dream about compassion and cooperation in our communities. I could see the buildings and the people of an ideal village, and I felt their dedication to social responsibility, to helping their neighbors. This is what makes a real community, what can transform our communities into a paradise, the way this world was intended. When we forget or are unaware, then people seek power, wealth, celebrity status, privilege. Instead of compassion and cooperation there exist hierarchies and the slavery of class differences.

Compassion, cooperation, caring for our neighbors, and our communal responsibilities are not matters of economics. They are attitudes of the heart and cannot be legislated or imposed from outside ourselves. They must be learned from within.

In this respect, it is not important whether or not a nation or community practices a particular economic or political system. The fruits of our talents and our labors should be shared throughout our community, dispensed after we have taken what we need for our families, dispensed with a sense of compassion and loving-kindness to others. The compassionate heart of each individual dispenses the products of his or her labor, not the particular economic system.

We receive and we give. In return we receive from others. Joy exists in the balance between giving and receiving.

When our communities are cooperative and compassionate, when they are responsible and kind, we can re-create a little bit of heaven upon the earth.

❧ CHAPTER EIGHT ❧

Changing the World

Co-existence and harmony . . . Everything must be bal-
anced. Nature is balanced. The beasts live in harmony. Hu-
mans have not learned to do that. They continue to destroy
themselves. There is no harmony, no plan to what they do.
It's so different in nature. Nature is balanced. Nature is en-
ergy and life . . . and restoration. And humans just destroy.
They destroy nature. They destroy other humans. They will
eventually destroy themselves.

In a meditation I saw that our planet took the form of a one-
room schoolhouse, the old-fashioned type where children in
grades one through twelve all occupy the same room and one
teacher teaches all the grades.

The school seemed to be in trouble. Younger students were
disturbing the more advanced. There was no harmony or cooperation. Even the schoolhouse itself was being defaced. I
knew that the school would cease to function if the chaos
were to persist.

Then I viewed several modern schools, each one nestled in
its own beautiful campus. An elementary school, a middle

school, and a senior high school. Each one was specialized and access was granted only to the assigned students. The classes were orderly but lacked the intensity and energy of the one-room schoolhouse.

Could our one-room schoolhouse, our planet, be evolving into disconnected components due to the chaos of society? Is the time coming for the more primitive students to be removed from the more advanced ones? For those still practicing violence, hatred, greed, and fear to be isolated from those who have mastered the traits of love, forgiveness, compassion, and kindness?

The dream ended, but the ending seemed vague. I knew that that model could be salvaged if cooperation, love, and harmony could somehow fill our one-room schoolhouse. In its ideal form, having the older students helping to teach the younger ones seemed beautifully efficient, one teacher with many assistants.

However, if disharmony, fear, and selfishness prevailed, the schoolhouse would have to be replaced with the safer, yet somehow more sterile, separate campuses.

The choice is still ours to make.

We all dream of a better life in a better society. However, it has become difficult to go through a complete day without becoming disillusioned, disappointed, and drained by the mean-spirited and selfish people who surround us. So many people seem to be interested only in their personal gain. They have become rude and arrogant, critical and insensitive. Not only do their actions drag us down, but most of us feel that there's nothing we can do to change this, that only those in power have the capacity to make a difference.

If we accept our task to *be* the enlightened beings of our planet, we can begin to change the world. Realistically, I think the changes will occur slowly as we begin to practice acts of kindness every day, doing little things to help make other people happier. Perhaps the answer is volunteering to help the less fortunate. Perhaps it's something as simple as being nice to someone, doing a kindness without asking for or expecting anything in return.

For years, television host and actress Oprah Winfrey has been advocating the practice of doing simple acts of kindness every day. These acts do not have to be expensive or complex. They can be nothing more than a pleasant smile, a spontaneous compliment, an assist to someone needing help. They can be a kind word, a sweet gesture, a caring action, a compassionate attitude, a shared joy, a helping hand. Little by little, step by step, a huge transformation of our society could begin. People would feel nourished by the kind gestures of others. Fearful attitudes and defensive insecurities would begin to melt away in the warmth of kindness.

Strangers must approach other strangers with these benevolent actions. Kindness and caring cannot be reserved only for our families and friends. Otherwise society will not change at all. We need to reach out to all the others, not merely those like us.

If we could get everyone to perform just a few acts of kindness each day, we could change the world. At least a good beginning could be made.

Our days would seem sweeter, less discouraging, and we would harbor more hope for the future. The model of kind and compassionate behavior toward our fellow human beings should be America's export and legacy, not greed-based business practices with money as the bottom line and ruthless, uncaring competition as the means to that end.

In addition, we would be role models for our children. They would learn the power and importance of being kind. They would learn that the actual number of people reached by their simple acts of kindness does not matter. The importance is in the doing.

Since the beginning of time, all the great teachers of humanity have preached love and compassion in our relationships and in our communities. They have not wasted their time instructing us how to accumulate excessive material wealth; they have not taught us to be mean, self-centered, rude, or arrogant.

A real master, a real teacher, a real guru will help you find your own path, showing you what is important for your spiritual evolution and what is not important or, even worse, what may be a hindrance or an obstacle.

Our job is to manifest their teachings in our everyday life. To be kind and nurturing, to practice loving acts.

There is no time schedule for changing the world. The only important thing is to begin. If it is true that a journey of a thousand miles begins with one step, then the first step is to let go of our fear and isolation and to begin to practice acts of kindness, whether random or planned, whether big or small, and to do this every day.

Changing the world from its current violent, competitive, and hate-filled nature will not happen through the efforts of only a few enlightened individuals, even if they are powerful world leaders. Rather, the day-to-day acts of kindness and compassion shared between people and within small groups can bring about the change to a more loving and kinder place. People have to understand that we are all equal, all the same, all striving for a little peacefulness, happiness, and security in our everyday lives. We can't keep fighting and killing each other.

Our children watch us closely. They model themselves on what they observe: our behavior, our values, and our attitudes. If we are hateful and violent, they will become the same. One of our most important tasks is to teach our children right values and right behavior beginning when they are infants, because babies, too, are observing us closely and they understand far more than we think.

I remember reading years ago about the Hopis, a Native American nation. In their educational system, if a student did not know the answer to a question asked of him or her in the classroom, no other student would raise a hand to answer that question. It was considered rude and uncivilized to embarrass or humiliate the first student. It was not important to impress the teacher with one's own brilliance, and it was thought to be barbaric to advance oneself at the expense of one's peers.

In the modern schools of our "civilized" Western world, of course, there would be a sea of hands upraised to take advantage of the unfortunate student who didn't know the answer. We are taught to profit at the expense of others, to climb over our peers on the way to the top. We are taught to be competitive and ruthless and to discount completely the feelings of those we are trampling. Forget the humiliation of the unknowing student. Here is our chance to impress the teacher.

These are the seeds of violence, and they are planted within us when we are very young. We can awaken and understand the nature of these weeds within, and uproot them. But this process requires awareness of our deeper nature, and it is not an easy process.

Years ago I taught a pharmacology course on alcohol and drugs of abuse to the second-year medical students at the University of Miami School of Medicine. The entire class attended this course.

Since I was more interested in what the students learned rather than their grades, I decided to take away the pressure of the final examination in this course. My belief was that the students could better concentrate on the subject matter if they were less anxious.

I was required by the university to administer a comprehensive final examination, which eventually consisted of 120 questions and a few essays. I announced to the students that at the last scheduled class before the final exam, I would tell them the questions and the essays that would appear the following week on the exam. We would devote that class to discussing the answers. In this way, I thought, not only would they really understand my course and its final exam, but they should all get A's.

I followed through on this plan.

As I began to review and grade their final exams, I was stunned. I fully expected everyone to get a near-perfect score. Instead, I was finding the usual bell-shaped curve, the standard distribution of grades where a small percentage gets A's, a similar percentage gets D's or F's, and the largest percentage winds up in the middle, with B's and C's. How could this be? I had *given* them the answers a week before the test.

One of the students, the daughter of a friend, had written a perfect examination. Perplexed, I asked her what happened.

"They didn't believe you," she answered. "They thought you were deceiving them, that you were giving them the wrong questions and answers and that you would change everything on the final." Fortunately, she had believed me.

These students were already conditioned by their culture to be cynical, distrustful, and incredibly competitive. These students would become our physicians of the next decade, our *healers*. Cynical, competitive, distrustful healers.

Our "civilized" culture is failing us. And to change things, we have to start with our children, showing them the importance of love and kindness, of faith and hope, of compassion and non-violence, treating each other with respect and dignity, not as bodies to be climbed over on the road to material success.

Gurus and presidents cannot do this for us. The responsibility lies with each of us, in our daily one-to-one encounters, to reach out and help each other, with acts of kindness, to not be concerned with what, if anything, comes back to us, to do this unselfishly.

In this way we can change the world.

If you do not have the opportunity to do great things, you can do small things in a great way.

Rejecting Violence and Hatred

We have no right to abruptly halt people's lives before they have lived out their karma. . . . We have no right. They will suffer greater retribution if we let them live. When they die and go to the next dimension, they will suffer there. They will be left in a very restless state. They will have no peace. And they will be sent back, but their lives will be very hard. And they will have to make up to those people that they hurt for the injustices that they did against them. . . . Only God can punish them, not us. They will be punished.

Violence is much more than just inflicting physical injury on another. Some forms of violence can be more devastating than the physical variety. It can be very subtle. Separating into "us" and "them" is an act of violence. Focusing on the differences between people rather than our commonality inevitably leads to violence, sooner or later.

We fear the "other." We project our self-hatred, our failures, and our faults onto them. We blame them for our problems rather than looking within ourselves. We attempt to solve our problems by "fixing" *them,* often with violence.

Thus country clubs with restricted memberships are violent places. It does not matter that the members wield no more than a golf club on a beautiful summer day on a tree-lined fairway. There is violence afoot. There is "we" and "them," all the others. The others are not like us. You cannot trust them. They are dangerous and to be feared.

When we reach out with caring and compassion to those who seem different from us, we conquer our fear and replace it with love. We overcome violence. We embrace our destiny.

I have heard that when the poet Maya Angelou hears a prejudiced remark against any group, she immediately and firmly says, "Stop it!" You will hear her majestic voice across a crowded room at a dinner party if she overhears a bigoted comment, story, or joke.

This is a wonderful technique. If we all did the same, bigotry and prejudice would diminish and hopefully fade away. But to say "Stop it!" requires great courage. We will have to command our families, friends, peers, bosses, and strangers to cease their angry behavior.

Although it may seem difficult, remember that we are swimming upstream against the current of love when we separate others as different. Love tells us that we are all connected, that we are all equal, that we are all the same.

You do not need to believe in reincarnation for past-life therapy to work. If you wish, you can believe the whole thing is metaphor. The imagery is rich, detailed, and therapeutic, whatever you believe.

In the spring of 1996 I was on the *Maury Povich* show. Prior to the live taping of the show, I regressed several people while the cameras filmed their experiences. One of these people was Jim, a musician in his late forties who was also a veteran of the war in Vietnam. He had been drafted unwillingly and he hated the prospect of killing, but he had had no choice and was compelled to be a soldier in this war.

I had never met Jim until just before his regression. I took a brief history, explained what we would be doing, and apologized for the intrusion of the television cameras and their lights. He told me that he had never been hypnotized before and that he had no personal experiences with past lives, but he was willing to try.

Within a few minutes, Jim was in a deep hypnotic trance and began to experience a powerful past-life scene. He was not at all distracted by the cameras or crew.

"I'm with an attachment of horse soldiers," he slowly began. "We're in the Dakotas someplace . . . we've . . . there are many Indians and we are being slaughtered . . . and I'm trying to convince my mates that . . . we are dying with honor . . . but . . . we are not." Tears were now streaming from his eyes. His grief and sadness were palpable.

"There is Gary," Jim added, a beautiful smile temporarily piercing the sadness. Gary is one of his closest friends in Jim's current life.

"You recognize him?" I asked softly.

"Yes," Jim answered with some relief, "my friend Gary."

"Is he one of you there?"

"Yes." Again the smile, yet the tears continued to fall.

"It's okay," I added, trying to assuage his grief. "We come around with the same people. . . . Do you survive this?"

"No!"

"What happens to you?"

"They take my hair," he answered grimly.

"What do you see?"

Jim's voice became even sadder. "Terrible carnage . . . Oh . . . the things we do."

I took him away from his death in that lifetime. "And now review, from the higher perspective, what did you learn from that experience, from that life?"

He was silent for a few moments. I observed his eyes moving back and forth, as if he were scanning images under his closed eyelids. Jim later told me that he was seeing a panorama of past-life scenes in which the horrors of war and unbridled violence were displayed to him. He was a participant in all of these episodes, sometimes as victim, sometimes as slayer, sometimes as bereaved survivor.

He sat motionless. I repeated my question. "Reviewing that lifetime from the higher perspective, what did you learn? What were the lessons?"

With teary eyes and in the softest voice, Jim answered, and I felt chills as I listened to his words.

"That life is holy and there is no reason *ever* to kill."

As Jim echoed the message Catherine had delivered from the Masters fifteen years earlier, my mind drifted back to him as a nineteen-year-old recruit objecting to the burgeoning war in Vietnam and to his discomfort in being a part of this war.

His was not a political or ideological objection. He must have remembered, at some deep emotional level, what he so tragically experienced in the Indian wars of the late nineteenth century.

Life is holy, and there is no reason ever to kill.

CHAPTER NINE

Finding the Light

For now, I just feel the peace. It's a time of comfort. The party must be comforted. The soul . . . the soul finds peace here. You leave all the bodily pains behind you. Your soul is peaceful and serene. It's a wonderful feeling . . . wonderful, like the sun is always shining on you. The light is so brilliant! Everything comes from the light! Energy comes from this light. Our soul immediately goes there. It's almost like a magnetic force that we're attracted to. It's wonderful. It's like a power source. It knows how to heal.

One of the most consistent findings in the research of NDEs is the experiencer's perception of a beautiful and comforting light. This light is not some neurochemical event occurring in an injured brain, but rather a wonderful glimpse into the world beyond. Often a loved relative who has previously died or a spiritual being is present at the light, offering advice, knowledge, and profound love. The person often becomes aware of details and events of which he or she had no previous knowledge. People have been told by their deceased loved ones where family jewels have been hidden and as yet undiscovered, where wills have been stored, and many other hidden facts. Later, after they have recovered from their illness or injury, they have found the articles, confirming the accuracy of the information received while they were unconscious or in a coma. A light "caused" by brain injury, as critics of the NDE have sometimes claimed, could not provide such precise validation.

Although certain details of the NDE may change from culture to culture, the perception of this beautiful light seems to be a universal phenomenon. In the United States, people undergoing an NDE often describe traversing a tunnel in order to reach the light. In Japan, crossing over a river or body of water to reach the light is a more common description. Nevertheless, whether moving through a tunnel or crossing a river, or traveling in any other manner, the light is a constant finding. So, too, is the sensation that accompanies it: There is peace and comfort at the light.

After conducting an intense two-day workshop in which many health-care professionals were participating, I received a letter from one of the professionals who had attended. She was thanking me for helping her and others to experience the beautiful light, the same light, I believe, that is seen and felt by people during the NDE and the after-death experience (ADE). Of course, people can touch this light in meditative or hypnotic states, in dreams, in spontaneous mystical experiences, and in many other ways.

She is now thirty-six years old, but her first experience with the light, still etched sharply in her memory, occurred when she was only fourteen. She wanted to share this with me, and I want to let you hear her words also, because her description is classical, accurate, and straightforward.

She was educated in a Catholic school system in Latin America. Spanish is her primary language, although her letter is written in English:

"I never knew about near- or after-death experiences, life before life and less about past lives. I never imagined that in ninth grade I would have something to tell about it."

During a spiritual retreat that her entire school class was attending, a priest taught them a few meditation and visualization techniques. He first had the group, which was lying on the floor, slow down their breathing. He then had them visualize themselves in a beautiful field, filled with flowers. At this point, the young woman's experience began to differ, becoming independent of the priest's gentle instructions.

"Birds were singing and we were enjoying our surroundings. We were instructed by the priest's sweet voice to continue our walk through the field but I found myself wrinkling my frown: I could no longer follow the priest's descriptions. I tried for three times and instead of being able to continue my walk, I always reached a well. I felt the priest's voice farther and farther, meanwhile it was still describing a field, without a well. . . .

"My body grew loose and I surrendered. At the same time I saw myself bending over to see what was inside the well but I fell into it. Then, it was no longer a well, but a tunnel. I had a little lamp in my right hand. I started walking through the tunnel: all was obscure except for the soft light of my lamp. After a while, I noted that the tunnel was curving slightly to the left and then, tiny light rays began to appear as I became closer. They grew large—and larger at each step of mine. I wanted fervently to see what was there.

"I reached the corner and then I saw it: Oh God, I was going to dismay! There was it! The most precious, brilliant and largest light I have ever seen! It is round and giant, incandescent, like the sun, but pure white. It seems solid but at the same time translucent! How can it be? (I wrote these few lines in present time because my soul knows this precious light exists and has existed always, for all of us.)

"I was afraid for a while but also irresistibly attracted by the light. Keeping my little lamp, I tried to penetrate the giant light, in front of me, agitating its glamorous beams. I must be inside it and know what was behind it! I wanted to be part of it! I could identify a masculine polarity in the light environment. . . .

"I was about to get in, when suddenly I heard a strong voice in my mind that told me: No, you can't trespass this light! I still remember the energy of the voice. It was a masculine, young voice but there was nobody visible. . . .

"There was an invisible barrier that kept me outside the light. Immediately to the voice, I felt a strong push in my chest which made me go backwards, flying in circles through the tunnel. . . . Suddenly the tunnel became again the well and then my fall was upwards! When I got out flying rapidly from the well I saw the sky and the field again and in that moment, I felt a blow inside my body, a sharp one, as if my soul had made a sudden arrival. It returned because it was not allowed to trespass the Light. . . ."

At this point she opened her eyes.

"Surprisingly, the priest was still describing the field of flowers and the students were still calm, with eyes closed. Nobody noted my arrival. . . ."

She was too anxious and moved by her experience to tell anyone. For many years she kept her entire experience with the light a very private secret.

Twelve years later she read a newspaper article describing the NDE of a four-year-old girl. She describes reading the article and becoming "overwhelmed with joy." She realized that the little girl could trespass the light because she had, for a moment, died.

"I cried a lot. I was no longer lonely. The light was not a fantasy. . . .

"I have never felt the love, peace, and divinity of my Light again. There is nothing comparable to it in our physical world. I miss it."

Now this woman works with dying patients in a hospital, helping them to make their transitions into the spiritual world, comforting and reassuring them because of her own spiritual experiences. Interestingly, she has also noticed many of the same phenomena as my youngest brother, Peter, and his wife, Barbra, who are oncologists and whose experiences with their dying patients are described in *Through Time Into Healing*.

She continues:

"I have the opportunity to be in the company of dying pa-tients. They 'see' their beloved parents or members of their family receiving them in their dimension or coming for them. These patients have described to me their visions and experi-ence before leaving. They are happy when they 'see' their mother or father or a beautiful being smiling at them. . . . I know they will enjoy their light.

"I need—and people need—to know more about how to manage and help people in the dying process because there is light: from the light we came and to the light we'll go. By the love and happiness that I felt from my light and perceived in my patients, I know love does not end with death. . . ."

And she is correct. The Light and Love never really end. They are intimately and eternally entwined.

Based on the knowledge I have gleaned from the Masters, the after-death experience is very similar. We still go to the light and receive the identical comfort, the same love, the soothing peace. The only difference is what happens next. In the NDE the person is returned to his or her physical body. In the ADE, the soul moves on, continuing to learn on the other side, in heaven, until returning here in a baby's body, incar-nating once again in the physical state, if that is necessary or chosen.

Lately there have been a few reports about people who have

experienced negative NDEs. In investigating this, I have found that sometimes the so-called negative NDE is not an actual NDE. Instead, the person who is injured has experienced a fluctuating level of consciousness during the trauma. He or she may become dimly aware of actual events taking place at a level of partial conscious awareness. I am not saying that there is no such thing as a negative NDE, just that there are very few cases reported and that some of these cases are not valid.

For example, I regressed a policeman who had been injured in a car accident while on duty. He described a "terrible" NDE in which his body had been pushed and probed and pierced by malevolent beings. In truth, as the regression proved, he had partially awakened while being transported by ambulance to the hospital emergency room. During the trip, the paramedics were administering emergency medical treatment, inserting intravenous lines for fluid replacement, injecting necessary medications, monitoring blood pressure, creating an airway to assist his breathing, and so on. In actuality, the "malevolent beings" were the emergency personnel who saved his life.

When you find the light, you find peace, comfort, and love. There is nothing negative about such a beautiful experience. I have never found hell, only different levels of ignorance. The more ignorance, the less light. Evil is a profound ignorance and a nearly complete absence of light.

It is rare to discover famous people or people of highly prominent stature during regressions to past lives. Henry was an exception. In his current life, he is a professor of engineering at a large Midwestern university. Very logical and rational in his thinking and actions, he had come to my workshop somewhat reluctantly, more to keep his wife company than to participate actively. As destiny would dictate, he now found himself in front of two hundred people, an ambivalent volunteer for an individual regression.

In some of the earlier group exercises, he had had some vivid childhood memories filled with detail and emotion. He was willing to explore even further.

Henry reached a depth of hypnosis that most do not reach. I remembered about never judging a book by its cover. Even engineers could allow themselves to go under deeply.

He went so deep that afterwards he experienced amnesia for the entire regression. With prompting, the memories he experienced returned, to some extent. Fortunately the entire regression was taped, so that afterwards he could re-experience everything.

His childhood memories were again filled with many details. Henry's memories under hypnosis were particularly vivid and profound.

At first, I took him back to the age of three, when his mother scolded him for darting into the street after a ball. He had almost been struck by a passing car. He could very acutely feel her anger and her relief, and he remembered his reactions to her conflicting emotions.

Then we moved into a past life, and his memories flooded back to him as he sat completely focused and in a deep trance, oblivious to the large audience, captivated by his recall. He was a general in the army of Rome.

"Do you become aware of something?" I asked, after bringing him into the state from which memories of past lives can emerge.

"Yes," he quickly responded. "I'm . . . I'm in a war. I'm in a fight. Uhh . . . I'm what looks like a Roman centurion. I'm wearing . . . I'm wearing the outfit of a general . . . and I'm with my men in the fight and I have a chariot driver and a chariot . . . and we're in the heat of battle and I'm throwing spears and killing people. And we're . . . we're . . . I'm directing the battle. We're driving this group of people . . . another army . . . it looks like a German army, looks like a north country army . . . into . . . we're driving them into a river, and then there's a steep wall on the other side of the river. . . ."

Henry did not need any prompting or questions from me. He continued to talk, like an officer, about the strategy of the battle.

"It looks like we're going to take the day very well." He went back to describing himself.

"I'm wearing a suit of armor. . . . The hat is bronze and has a plume . . . there's a faceplate on the helmet. . . . I have a breastplate made of metal . . . and I have a short dress-like . . . armor that comes from my waist and goes about halfway to the knees. . . .

"As I'm throwing the spears, I'm aware that someone has thrown one at me, and I'm . . . not afraid!" he added with some surprise at his lack of fear.

"And it hits me, it hits me right here," he elaborated, point-ing at his lower right abdomen. "And I have this new metal in my armor . . . and I'm not afraid of spear points made of rocks and . . . and just sharpened points. My armor is way too strong. . . .

"After that I drove . . . I gave the chariot . . . we moved to the rear because we didn't have to be in the battle anymore . . . and we let the battle continue. We watched it from the hill . . . safely. . . . Augustus wants the generals to enter the battle but not stay with the battle . . . especially if we're winning big."

He now became silent. Clearly the battle was being won. I decided to move him ahead in time. I directed him to go to the end of that lifetime. The silence continued for a few more moments, and then he began to speak again.

"I'm . . . I'm a rich man, even though I started out just a poor boy, but I'm a rich man, and I have land . . . and I see lots of columns. And I'm in the Senate. I wear a robe with a purple stripe. I'm a senator."

"So you have power?" I asked.

"Yes, yes, I do have some power," he added, "but not as much as Caesar. I just mainly . . . I'm retired now, and I don't fight anymore. I just mainly stay on my land in Sicily and just . . . farming and raising sheep. And I see Caesar every once in a while when he comes to Syracuse."

"Are you ready to leave that time . . . or is there more?" I asked.

"I see myself dying," he responded. "I'm a very old man and . . . I'm on a hard bed-like surface . . . and I can see people around me hurrying . . . hurrying . . . hurrying. And I look up with my eyes, but my head stays on my bed . . . and I see . . . my wife . . . and then I die." He grew silent.

"What do you become aware of next?" I inquired.

"I see . . . I see myself. . . . I'm a young man again. I see myself looking down at the room. I'm pleased. . . . I'm happy and pleased, and I can see myself."

"And there is a call . . . or someone is calling me . . . and there shines a bright yellow light . . . a yellow light, very strong. I can't look into the light . . . but there is a voice in the light calling me, so I walk into the light. . . .

"Being in the light feels very nice, feels like warm energy all around your body. It feels very comfortable, feels like the ideal . . . the ideal climate. I'm still wearing my senator's robes . . . but I'm young . . . I'm young again." Once more, he paused.

"Is there any more that you can tell us from this state?" I asked.

"What happens next . . . I don't know . . . I don't know. . . . This is the last that I can remember right now," he slowly responded.

I brought Henry out of his deep trance.

"How do you feel?" I asked.

"I feel good," he answered. "Are we going to start?" The last conscious memory Henry had was my beginning to hypnotize him about forty-five minutes earlier.

A week after this experience, a close friend of Henry's told me that Henry was feeling wonderful, that his regression had brought him more peace and happiness than he had ever felt before, at least in this life.

I smiled. So many fears disappear when you can so directly and so deeply be reminded of your divinity, of your immortality. Henry had no doubt that he had lived many centuries ago in Rome. Yet even more than the memories of our past lifetimes, when one remembers the beautiful light we encounter after we leave our physical bodies, not only do fears vanish, but a sense of transcendent joy and comfort almost overwhelms us. This is such a loving light. It nourishes our souls. Henry had felt the light.

His light was yellow. Sometimes I hear the light described as golden. Sometimes as indescribable, as all colors simultaneously. But always as comforting and loving.

Death is not what most of us believe. Death is the shedding of the physical body as the immortal soul progresses to the other side. In this sense there is no death, only life and love. The light is one more manifestation of this universal, timeless, all-encompassing love.

Researchers into the NDE, such as Dr. Raymond Moody and Dr. Elisabeth Kübler-Ross, often describe a "life-review" session. One or several wise and loving beings assist you in reviewing the events in your life. Particular interest is paid to your relationships, how you dealt with others.

From my research with patients remembering their deaths in previous lifetimes, I find that the death experience is very much the same for all of them. The life review is done in a loving way, without judgment or criticism. However, you feel emotions deeply, both yours and the other person's, and thus you learn at a profound level.

For example, if you genuinely helped another person in a time of need, you feel that person's gratitude and love coming back to you.

But if you hurt or injured others, emotionally or physically, you experience their anger as well as their hurt.

What a wonderful learning opportunity.

Afterwards, you and your committee, which is comprised of the loving guides, masters, angels, and others who have helped to guide you over eons of time, plan your next life, so that you can rectify the wrongs you have done.

We are always growing and learning.

When you no longer need to reincarnate, when you have learned all your lessons and cleared all debts, then you are given a choice. You can return voluntarily in order to help humankind in loving service. Or you can stay on the other side, helping from that state. In both cases, you continue to progress along the heavenly dimensions.

Other Dimensions

"Humans always think of themselves as the only beings. This is not the case. There are many worlds and many dimensions . . . many, many more souls. . . ."

"There are many souls in this dimension. I am not the only one. We must be patient. That is something I never learned, either. . . . There are many dimensions. . . ."

I asked her whether she had been here before, whether she had reincarnated many times.

*"I have been to different planes at different times. Each
one is a level of higher consciousness. What plane we go to
depends upon how far we've progressed. . . ."*

There are many more people than ever before on this planet.
But there are many more souls than people. This is not the
only world. Souls exist in many dimensions. They are attracted
to this planet in increasing numbers because our planet, one
of many schools, is a *very* popular school. There is so much to
learn here.

When I talk about other dimensions, I mean other energetic states or even different levels of consciousness, not necessarily other planetary systems or galaxies. Heaven can be
considered another dimension, since energy transformation
beyond three-dimensional consciousness is undoubtedly involved.

I believe that the energy of love has physical and extra-
physical properties and can exist in all of the various dimensions. Love is the connecting substance that unites all of the
dimensions and the different planes beyond the physical.

Within one dimension or plane, many sub-levels exist. Another way of saying this is that there are many levels in heaven.
We progress step-wise along these levels as we become more
and more enlightened.

In one sense, we are all aliens. None of us began on this
planet. This planet is more like a high school. It is not the low-
est level, nor the highest. But this is a very popular school.
When we graduate, we will go elsewhere.

But in all of the universes, souls are all the same.

Robert, a young waiter who had experienced many hardships
in his current life, carried around a kind of chronic melan-
choly. There was very little that could produce joy in his life.
He had financial problems, and he tended to shy away from

relationships because he had been hurt so often in his child-hood. Very stoical, his face rarely betrayed his emotions.

In a deep trance state, he entered a garden or tropical jun-gle scene. Immediately he began to cry with tears of joy and happiness. He could barely talk. Such a display of emotion was uncharacteristic for him.

"How do you feel?" I asked him.

"It's just . . . just a jungle scene . . . it's just *home* . . . home," he responded very slowly. His voice was filled with emotion.

"You seem to be feeling something profound. What is it?"

"A rejoicing . . ." Tears continued to flow down his cheeks. He couldn't really talk, so I awakened him after a few more minutes. My hope was that he could describe more from the conscious state, where the level of emotion would not be so profound and overwhelming. After a few minutes more, he had regained some of his composure.

"What did you experience?" I asked.

"I just saw almost a paradise-like scene . . . real lush and shining. . . . There was nobody else there. . . ."

"Why do you think this was so emotional?" I asked, but he had difficulty answering. He was still feeling deeply moved by his experience.

Finally he began to talk, although briefly.

"I feel like it's inevitable that I will be back there sometime. I get the feeling that I know I've been there before, and that it's some place I'm going . . . so I don't want to rush anything and I want to feel the steps."

Later that week he explained the sense of familiarity, the feeling of incredible peace and safety, that he experienced dur-ing the regression. He still had difficulty finding the words to describe his visit to the paradise-like jungle. This time, his dif-ficulty was due not only to the overwhelming obstacle of pro-found emotion, but because mere words could not do justice to the beauty, joy, and majesty of the experience. It was ineffable.

I believe Robert had a spiritual experience rather than a past-life memory.

The intensity of his joy coupled with the characteristics of the evoked scene and the relative paucity of detail and progression along a lifetime all indicate this to me. In a small way, he re-experienced the joy of going home. Earth, the three-dimensional world, is not really our true home. We are spiritual beings, and our true home is a spiritual one, a timeless place that many call heaven.

CHAPTER TEN

Healers

We must share our knowledge with other people. . . . We all have abilities far beyond what we use.

You develop through relationships. There are some with higher powers who have come back with more knowledge. They will seek out those who need the development and help them.

In this one-room schoolhouse we call the earth, we do not learn all of our lessons simultaneously. For example, we may have already mastered the course in compassion and charity, but we may only be beginners when it comes to patience or forgiveness. We may be graduate students in faith and hope, but kindergartners in anger or non-violence.

Similarly, we may carry over skills and talents learned in earlier incarnations, skills we have mastered, yet we may be novices in other areas. We have among us many who have mastered certain courses and skills, and they are here to share their knowledge with us, the students. In other areas, our roles may reverse.

Thus we are all teachers and we are all students, and we must share our knowledge with each other.

Many physicians have chosen to be doctors in order to manifest their healing abilities, to help and to teach others. Conversely, a wise physician will always be open to learning from his or her patients. The patient might be able to teach the physician about love, about courage, about inner peace, or any of the other lessons we are here to learn. Both physician and patient benefit.

Late one afternoon a patient of mine came into her session complaining of an infected tetanus shot. Her arm was swollen, hot, painful, and hard in the area of the shot. She had just met her internist in the hallway of the hospital on her way to my office. He instructed her to come to his office the next morning in order to begin a course of antibiotic treatment.

"Those things need antibiotics," he had said, "or else they get worse."

I decided to try helping her with hypnosis. She quickly drifted into a deep hypnotic state, and I instructed her to bring healing light to the affected area of her arm. I had her visualize an increased blood flow to the infection, cleaning the area, carrying away damaged cells and eliminating damaging bacteria. She vividly imagined healthy new cells and the complete absence of disease.

By the end of the session, the pain had disappeared and the infected area was not as hot. I was not surprised, because hypnosis has long been used as a technique to diminish pain. By bedtime, the swollen area was only half as large. By the next morning, her arm had entirely returned to normal, and there was no evidence of an infection.

She went to her physician anyway.

"What happened to your arm?" he exclaimed. "Those things never clear up on their own!"

"It must have been a spontaneous remission," she answered, keeping her secret.

She knew he could accept that explanation. He was close-minded to alternative or complementary medicine. If she had said she was healed through guided imagery under hypnosis, he would have scoffed.

No remission of illness is truly spontaneous. We may not be consciously aware of the underlying mechanisms, but strong healing forces have been "secretly" at work healing the damage.

I knew Dr. Bernie Siegel long before he became the well-known author of several marvelous books about the mind-body connection. *Love, Medicine and Miracles* and *Peace, Love and Healing* are two of his international best-sellers.

Bernie was an attending surgeon at Yale–New Haven Hospital, in private practice in New Haven, Connecticut, when I was a medical student at Yale on my surgery rotation in the late 1960s. I chose to observe and assist the private surgeons because they were generally faster and funnier than the full-time academic staff, who tended to be more authoritarian, didactic, and rigid. Bernie and his associate, Dr. Richard Selzer, who has also written several popular books, were especially funny. Their patients were not the only ones who wound up in stitches. The surgeons made jokes, recited risqué poetry, told stories and vignettes—these were really funny guys. In addition, both were excellent technical surgeons, and I learned a lot about surgery.

At this time, none of us realized that some patients, even though they were under general anesthesia, were also listening to the conversations, jokes, and bantering. We know this now. I spoke to Bernie recently after he had conducted a workshop in Miami. We decided that the jokes and bantering at that time were okay. At the worst, the patient might have felt some concern, thinking: Dr. Siegel, why are you joking? Pay more attention to my body. This is *important* to me.

Better that the patient overhear his surgeon making jokes than giving dire and calamitous predictions about the patient's chances, or speculating about permanent disabilities the surgery may cause. Such pronouncements might convince the patient to give up rather than to face enormous obstacles and handicaps.

There is a more profound chemistry for physicians to experience than those found in blood tests and laboratories.

Many physicians are so busy, stressed, self-absorbed, afraid, or greedy that they do not take the time to listen to their patients, to have a relationship with their patients. This is a tragic state of affairs both for the physician and the patient. The physician denies himself or herself the satisfaction of knowing the patient on a personal basis and loses the opportunity to learn from the therapeutic encounter. Without the real gratification that comes from a person-to-person connection, the practice of medicine becomes sterile and mechanistic. The physician begins to feel constantly rushed and behind schedule. Depression and early burnout are common results. The patient also feels rushed and uncared for, of interest merely as an illness or an organ (or even worse, as a dollar) to the doctor rather than as a whole person or even as a friend. The patient's dignity and humanity are eroded.

All physicians can be deeply touched if they take the time to listen to and to learn from their patients. Many doctors have told me about their more "unusual" cases, cases that have touched upon areas not yet taught in medical schools.

An eminent plastic surgeon in the Miami area told me about a most remarkable case. Months had passed, but the surgeon's face still reflected his amazement.

A patient of his had been involved in a serious automobile

accident. She had sustained massive head trauma, facial fractures, and other internal injuries. Although emergency surgery had been scheduled, the patient was not expected to live.

As the surgeon was preparing the family for the inevitably fatal outcome, the patient floated out of her body. Although the family-doctor conference was taking place in a part of the hospital far from where the medical team was working on her injuries, she found them and overheard the conversation, helplessly watching her family's grief and despair. She looked down from her ethereal body.

"I'm not dead!" she yelled, but nobody seemed to hear her. Frustrated that her cries went unheard and angry that her family was being told she would die, she floated back to her physical body. With the help of excellent medical care combined with the strength of her will to survive, she had what the doctor called a "miraculous" recovery. "Nobody recovers from injuries like hers," he kept saying. Later on, she was able to repeat the conversation the doctor had had with her family. Not only had she avoided physical death, but she was somehow able to accelerate the healing process dramatically. Her bones and tissues mended at many times normal speed.

An elderly lady, blind from diabetes, suffered a cardiac arrest during her stay in the hospital where I was the chairman of the psychiatry department. She was unconscious as the resuscitation team tried to revive her. According to her later report, she floated out of her body and stood near the window, watching, as the doctors administered medicines through hastily inserted intravenous tubes. She observed, without any pain whatsoever, as they thumped on her chest and pumped air into her lungs. During the resuscitation, a pen fell out of her doctor's pocket and rolled near the same window where her out-of-body spirit was standing and watching. The doctor eventually walked over, picked up the pen, and put it back in his pocket. He then rejoined the frantic effort to save her. They succeeded.

A few days later, she told her doctor that she had observed the resuscitation team at work during her cardiac arrest. "No," he soothingly reassured her. "You probably were hallucinating because of the anoxia [lack of oxygen to the brain]. This can happen when the heart stops beating."

"But I saw your pen roll over to the window," she replied. Then she described the pen and other details of the resuscitation.

The doctor was shocked. His patient had not only been comatose during the resuscitation, but she had also been blind for many years.

We have more ways to see than only with our eyes.

One of the hospital's doctors called me in to see a patient of his who had awakened screaming and highly agitated in the recovery room following major surgery. She had been given general anesthesia and was hence unconscious throughout the procedure, and her breathing was controlled by the anesthesiologist. During the surgery, the surgeons had experienced some difficulty with her blood pressure and heart rhythm.

During the surgery she had floated above the surgeons working on her body. The patient became alarmed when her blood pressure and heart rhythm became abnormal. She noted the concern in the anesthesiologist's voice and floated over to him and read his notations on her chart.

Upon awakening in the recovery room, panicked because of these abnormalities, she was able to tell me what had been written on her chart during the surgical procedure. The patient was unconscious throughout the procedure, yet even if she had awakened, she would not have had the opportunity to see her chart; the anesthesiologist was writing in back of her, a yard or so behind her head.

An emergency room physician at a nearby hospital stood in

line at a book signing for more than thirty minutes to tell me his story.

A patient of his had experienced the sudden onset of ana-phylactic shock after she was stung by a bee. This is a poten-tially lethal allergic reaction that causes a massive drop in blood pressure. Even though heroic lifesaving measures had been started when she entered the emergency room, the doc-tor was convinced that the patient was dying.

This patient later reported that she had floated alongside her own body as she was wheeled into the hospital. She over-heard, and later repeated, all of the discussions, the barking of orders, the swearing, the expectations, and the anxious re-marks of the emergency room staff. She "saw" their faces, their clothes, and who was doing what, even though she was co-matose. She also had a miraculous recovery and the doctor later validated the accuracy of her observations and her recall of the events and conversations, some of which took place in different rooms.

I have heard these and other stories of clinical accounts of patients with near-death and out-of-body experiences from so many physicians that I cannot explain them away on medical or physiological grounds. These are highly educated, logical, and skeptical doctors, rigorously trained in medical schools. All were telling me that, beyond a doubt, their patients, although unconscious, had left their bodies and "heard" and "observed" events at a distance.

I no longer believe that these events are rare. Most patients are reluctant to tell their doctors because they are afraid that the doctor will assume that they had been hallucinating or think them strange or crazy. Why take the risk?

And why should the doctors take the risk of sharing these experiences? Many psychiatrists have been afraid to talk in public about their experiences with regressions. I have had phone calls and letters from hundreds of psychiatrists (and thousands more from psychologists, social workers, hypnotherapists, nurse-clinicians, and other therapists) telling me that they have been doing regressions to past lives "in the privacy of my office," or "in secret, without telling any of my colleagues," for the past five or ten or sometimes twenty years. Here are thousands of cases, storehouses of valuable details, data, and facts. Here are clinical accounts, many of which can be validated and confirmed. More proof! The letters describe detailed accounts of past-life recall, of patients recalling names, dates, and details of lifetimes in other cities, countries, or continents. Some patients have found their "old" names in the official records of places they have never even heard of, let alone visited, in this lifetime. Some have found their own tombstones.

The risk of going public is potentially severe. Doctors fear that their hard-earned reputations, their practices, the security of their families, even their social relationships, will all be jeopardized. I understand this trepidation. It took me years to gather the courage to publish my findings.

Yet it is because they are credible that physicians have the opportunity to reinforce these truths by coming forward with their findings. In doing so, they can benefit millions of people, and they can also benefit themselves. Sharing truths, whether about out-of-body and near-death experiences, cases of unusual or "miraculous" healing, or examples of past-life memories and therapy, is just as important as sharing information on "traditional" medical research. The more we know, the more people we can help. Moreover, in learning these truths through their own patients and experiences, physicians will feel happier and more satisfied and fulfilled in their personal and professional lives.

I know! I have been there.

Most of the stories from physicians are about NDEs and out-of-body experiences (OBEs). It is less likely that they would be in a position to encounter past-life experiences. This makes sense, however, because physicians are often treating very ill patients.

Whether people have an OBE, NDE, or past-life experience, the healing that occurs is similar. Patients often find that their lives have been transformed in a positive way. Physical and emotional healing may be dramatically accelerated.

The element common to all these experiences is the existence of the consciousness beyond the physical body or brain. This consciousness is expanded upon leaving the physical body. Colors and sounds are more vivid. The purpose of our soul's journey becomes more clear. Our spiritual nature is manifest; and in those moments we understand we are immortal beings of wisdom, infinite love, and compassion. Paradoxically, during this seeming separation, the mind-body connection seems to be strengthened, or at least a bit more in our control. Healing occurs as the mind, through its awareness and will, sends energy to those parts of our body that need repair.

For centuries, many Asian cultures, including the Chinese, Japanese, and Korean, have recognized the healing energies and currents that course through our bodies. They have worked with these energies and even mapped out the characteristics of energy flow and intensity. The Chinese call this energy *chi* or *qi,* the Japanese *ki.* These cultures have fostered experts on the mind-body connections, and I have been fortunate enough to work with some of them.

On two separate occasions I have had the opportunity to regress physicians from mainland China. Both were also masters of energy work and healing.

The first doctor was the subject of a study at the physics department at New York University. NYU asked me to be a liaison since I was a physician who was well known in China, where my books have been best-sellers.

The Chinese physician spoke no English, so we worked with an interpreter. Curious whether my techniques were similar to those of the master with whom he had studied as a youth, he asked that we attempt a regression. He slipped into a deep hypnotic state and experienced an interesting past-life memory.

Afterwards he commented that our techniques were indeed very similar. Then he asked if I had seen and experienced his past-life scenes, as if we were watching the same movie together.

"No," I answered. "Sometimes I get premonitions of what is going to happen, but I don't actually see what is happening in your mind."

"A pity," he replied through the interpreter. "My master could."

On the other occasion, a famous Chinese physician visited me in Miami and demonstrated a powerful Qi Gong healing. In return, she requested a past-life regression, and I agreed. She also spoke no English, but she traveled with a translator.

She went under very deeply. Within a few minutes she was vividly recalling a past-life scene in San Francisco more than one hundred years ago. She began speaking fluent English during the recall.

The interpreter, a trained professional, did not miss a beat. He immediately turned to me and began translating into Chinese. I stared at him for a moment, and then pointed out that he did not need to do that. The shocked look on his face conveyed his realization.

He knew she could not speak a word of English.

Psychoanalysis and psychoanalytically oriented psychotherapies are in their death throes. Techniques are outmoded, slow, and ineffective. Language has become encrusted, formalized, impenetrable. There is no lifeblood in psychotherapy these days, just arid and monolithic structures, just dust. Not enough people can be reached, especially one at a time. And to even these few, the worn-out, agonizingly slow, cold, and distant approach of these therapies will not suffice. One neurosis is replaced by another in traditional therapy. Outward "functioning," not inner peace and joy, is the measure of success. There is no transformation of the individual or of society.

The economic disintegration is evident. People cannot afford the fifty-minute hour four to six times a week for anywhere from three to fifteen years. Most cannot even afford to come in weekly. Insurance policies and managed care are drastically limiting payments.

Freud and his disciples made important contributions to our understanding of the functioning of the mind, the existence of the unconscious, childhood sexuality, and to dream analysis, but psychoanalysis has no spiritual roots and cannot release the spiritual nature of humans. Freud may not have seen his theories as terminal, but his disciples set them in stone.

Jung was a maverick and ahead of his time. He understood the mysterious, the spiritual, the supernatural. But he was surrounded by those chiseling in stone.

One major flaw of psychoanalysis and related traditional psychotherapy is the concept of ego repair. The ego is the "I," the executive function, the part of us that has to integrate and deal with everyday reality. It is our ordinary or "everyday" mind. The everyday mind is logical, rational, has to make decisions, uses thought and memory, plans for and worries about the future, and broods about the past. It is always making judgments, putting thoughts in our minds, reviewing the data of the past, asking questions like "But suppose . . . ?" and "What if . . . ?" Unfortunately, most psychotherapists are con-

stantly trying to repair our damaged egos. Our egos get
bruised, as they see it, by our critical and dysfunctional parents, our childhood traumas, our inescapable physical limitations as an infant, and so on. These therapists are always
soothing or repairing or even hyper-inflating our egos. In
truth we must learn to go beyond our egos.

But surely we will fall apart! How can we function and survive without our egos, our everyday minds, in control? The
answer is very simple. Traditional therapists are stuck in the illusion that functioning is the ultimate goal, but inner peace
and joy are actually much more important. If we can gradually decrease our concern with functioning and fitting into
our sick society, with acquiring things and worrying about
what other people are thinking about us, then we can gradually begin to increase our inner joy. Our minds trap us in the
past and in the future. Constantly worrying, analyzing, and
thinking, our egos prevent us from truly being in the present,
from climbing out of the rut of habit and conditioning. How
can we *see* things as they really exist in the present when our
past conditioning and assumptions, our preconceived ideas, bi-
ases, and prejudices, are constantly getting in our way? We
must control this ego in order to save ourselves and, ultimately, our world.

Psychoanalysis is essentially unspiritual. It is a sterile discipline. It teaches nothing about immortality, the survival of the
soul after physical death, about the real values in life. It stops
short of the real questions and issues. When it does work, it is
because the therapist connects with the patient on a truly caring, compassionate level. The relationship is what heals.

Biological psychiatry often falls short too. The new medicines to treat depression, mood swings, and psychotic states are
means to an end, not the end itself. Too many psychiatrists
prescribe medications and do nothing else. This is a tremendous waste. The medicines can help to make the patient *acces-*

sible to the psycho-spiritual therapy that must then take place. To leave out the therapy is to leave out the entire essence of the treatment.

In addition, there are problems with most of the hundreds of self-help books out there. I wish therapy were so simple, a "quick-fix," but it is not. To reach a happy, satisfied, and joyful state is difficult. To maintain the state, once reached, is even more challenging.

It is hard work to stay out of the rut. To search within, to truly understand oneself, to foster a sense of detachment and perspective—these are difficult tasks and they require patience and much practice. The journey is arduous and long, but well worth it. To be truly happy requires an understanding of life and of death, and a loving, forgiving, spiritual nature. Introspection, meditation, loving service, kindness, and charity— these are some of the steps along the way. Practicing forgiveness of yourself and others, non-violence and good deeds, working to eliminate anger, fear, greed, self-centeredness, and false pride—these are yet more steps.

Many therapists refuse to consider using regression techniques, particularly regression to past lifetimes. As many clinicians have repeatedly documented, psychological and physical improvement, remissions, and cures often occur with dramatic rapidity. Whether in one session or ten, the results of regression therapy are long-lasting and life-changing. Spiritual growth, wisdom, and inner peace usually accompany the clinical improvement.

I believe there are two primary reasons why the medical and psychotherapeutic establishments are reluctant even to evaluate, let alone accept, these relatively rapid, inexpensive, and safe new approaches. The first is fear. The second reason is economic.

We all know that fear of the unknown closes people's minds. They become unwilling to take reasonable risks, to try out the new. Therapists who are afraid to learn new techniques, despite the greater efficacy, economy, and speed of these new techniques, do a great disservice to their patients and to themselves. Because of fear, their instinct to help is perverted. The real question remains: Why are they afraid?

The economic reasons stem from the rapidity of results and the long-lasting nature of the cures. As frightening as it is to reduce mental health to a business, fewer sessions and a lower relapse rate mean many fewer dollars.

The joy and happiness that practicing spiritual psychotherapy can bring to therapists and their patients far outweigh these anxieties and fears.

As I mentioned, holistic and complementary healing techniques are sweeping across the medical establishment, reinvigorating the health-care scene. Chiropractic procedures, hypnotherapy, acupuncture, herbal medicines, bioenergetics, meditation, yoga, massage, and many other alternative healing modalities are moving toward the mainstream. Eventually a balanced blend of traditional medical models and a complementary approach will allow health-care professionals to heal the whole person, his or her body, mind, and spirit.

This invigorating breeze is not a hurricane simply blowing away the old. A harmony must be established among the traditional and the holistic techniques so that an individualized program can be formulated based upon the symptoms and needs of the particular patient.

If our healers, traditional or otherwise, can keep open-minded about "other" techniques, if they can practice the healing arts with compassion, skill, and mindfulness, and, most importantly, if they can treat the spirit as well as the body, then we can truly enjoy optimal health.

CHAPTER ELEVEN

Teachers

We also must learn not to just go to those people whose vibrations are the same as ours. It is normal to feel drawn to somebody who is on the same level that you are. But this is wrong. You must also go to those people whose vibrations are wrong . . . with yours. This is the importance . . . in helping . . . these people.

Our path is an inward one. This is the more difficult path, the more painful journey. We bear the responsibility for our own learning.

Wise teachers walk among us to show us the way, to ease the burdens along our spiritual path. Unfortunately, there are also many pretenders in our midst. Whether driven by pride, ego, greed, insecurity, or other selfish forces, they masquerade as teachers or gurus. They tell you what to do when they themselves don't have a clue. Clearly it is dangerous to follow such people, but how do we, as loving, open-minded individuals, separate the wheat from the chaff?

The key to discerning a real teacher from a pretender is to

follow your own intuitional wisdom. Do the teachings feel right to you? Are they loving, compassionate, non-violent, and fear-reducing? Do they include all other groups, all other humans as equals, as divine souls on the same path of destiny? Do they teach that one is no better than the other, that we are all rowing the very same boat? And do they acknowledge that though they can point out the way, they cannot "bring you" to spiritual fulfillment? Only you can reach your goal, because ultimately our journey home is an inward journey, a personal return.

Gurus can teach us skills and techniques. They can increase our understanding of life, death, and the spiritual planes. They can help to remove fears and obstacles. They can point out the doorway, but it is we who must go through the door.

Because the kingdom of heaven really exists *within* us, all joy and happiness come from within ourselves. We are not going to be rescued by someone else. As we experience true love and become enlightened, we will "save" ourselves.

Do you remember Flip Wilson, the wonderful comedian whose character Geraldine would do something "sinful" or selfish and then stand, hands on hips, and declare, "The Devil made me do it"? What a powerful projection. The idea that we are not responsible for our actions is an attractive one. It's awfully expedient to have some outside force to blame.

Some people blame fate. Although our lives travel along predetermined courses, fate is not responsible for our actions. And just as we must take complete responsibility for our negative and harmful behavior, so we need to take responsibility for our positive and loving behavior. No one else can do this for us.

No devil can harm you, and ultimately no guru can save you.

At a conference in Seattle where we were both teaching, I

heard the brilliant scholar and mystic Jean Houston warn about the danger of blindly following a guru.

"Remember," Jean said, "that guru is spelled 'Gee, you are you.'"

To my surprise and amusement, the next day *Vanity Fair* magazine named me the guru of Miami.

Once, at the end of the day, after my staff had left and the office had become quiet in the fading twilight, I sank into a deep meditative state. The day had ended on a frustrating note, and over the years I have found that meditating in a quiet area around the time of dusk soothes me.

My last patient that day had once again been unsuccessful in recovering any past-life memories. She had a very difficult time even relaxing and reaching deeper levels of consciousness. She always seemed to become restless at a certain point in the relaxation exercise. She would spontaneously return to waking consciousness and implore me to move her into a deeper level.

This woman is an avid reader and has read many metaphysical books and articles. She had attended numerous New Age seminars and workshops. She read about and witnessed the experiences of others, but she had no such experiences herself. And she desperately wanted to have her own personal experiences.

Lately she had been reading books about Sai Baba, the famous spiritual teacher from India, and she was considering a trip to India to visit him. Perhaps he could help her past her impasse.

I knew immediately that the messages and images flowing into my awareness while meditating that quiet evening pertained to her, my frustrated patient.

"Our task is not to follow Sai Baba," the message began, "but to *be* Sai Baba." I patiently waited for more.

"He is love in action, and you must be love in action. Her task in this life is to manifest loving service."

At this point, I began to see visual images of my patient's past lives, a kaleidoscope of images flashing before me. I saw many monastic lifetimes, and the answer to her frustration became clear to me.

She had lived many lives in solitude, in monasteries and in convents. She had mastered the art of going within, of meditating to deep inner levels. But, in the current life, she needed to live in the real world, among real people with real problems—to help these people. She needed to express her love and compassion in a public way.

And so a block had been placed on her meditation. Otherwise she would have reverted back to her old pattern of going only to inner states and she would have neglected her soul's purpose in this life. She would not be acting in the world, among the people.

At her next session, I told her about this meditation experience. She seemed to be immediately relieved, as if a huge weight had been lifted from her shoulders. She was not a failure; she was merely being guided along her chosen path in this life.

"Been there, done that" became her attitude about deep daily meditations. She began to volunteer in programs to help the poor and homeless, and she raised money for many charities. She felt happier than she had ever been.

Ironically, as she continued and expanded her charitable work, her ability to meditate began to return. She felt balanced, and her work with me came to a natural end.

"Our task is not to follow Sai Baba, but to *be* Sai Baba."

Everything will be clear to you in time. But you must have a chance to digest the knowledge that we have given to you already.

Years ago I spoke at a huge New Age meeting held in Los Angeles. Nearly forty thousand people registered and paid money to hear a tremendous assortment of speakers ranging from serious university professors and scientists to upstart opportunists hawking their wares. Physicists rubbed elbows with cult leaders. I became very confused. How do you sort out these people? Can you tell anything by their credentials? I felt like protecting all forty thousand.

First, it was easy to rule out the speakers who came from other galaxies. Second, 95 percent of the channelers were either communicating with their subconscious minds or were consciously producing their "messages from beyond." Third, I could ignore the tons of crystals being sold from hundreds of booths in the convention area. However, the music was nice, the people extraordinarily friendly.

I attended many lectures and workshops. Some of the speakers were brilliant, particularly the scientists; clearly they had a great deal to teach. Others were terrible. As I listened to speakers make one outlandish statement after another without any confirming information or studies, I tried to gauge the audience's reaction. Much to my dismay, I saw many people just nodding their heads, accepting without thought or challenge.

Most of the forty thousand had come because they wanted something more in their lives. Many wanted some confirmation of their own psychic and intuitive experiences. They wanted new experiences and insights. They wanted to grow. They wanted to be stimulated. They wanted what we all want: a way to find and experience joy and peace.

But most had left their critical minds at home.

I wish I could have addressed the entire forty thousand. I wanted to tell them to stop looking for external answers, for quick fixes and quick cures. I wanted to tell them to look within. Now I will give advice I would like to have given to the forty thousand people so eager to change their lives.

≫ CHAPTER TWELVE ≪

Psychics and Mediums

Learning in the spiritual state is much faster, far accelerated from learning in the physical state. But we choose what we need to learn. If we need to come back to work through a relationship, we come back. If we are finished with that, we go on. In spiritual form you can always contact those that are in physical state if you choose to. But only if there is importance there . . . if you have to tell them something that they must know.

Sometimes you can appear before that person . . . and look the same way you did when you were here. Other times you just make a mental contact. Sometimes the messages are cryptic, but most often the person knows what it pertains to. They understand it's mind-to-mind contact.

From my research and experience with thousands of patients and my investigation into the abilities of some of the most talented psychic mediums in the world, it appears that we are not alone in the universe. Beyond our physical dimension, the "unseen" world appears to be populated by a myriad of spirits of varying abilities and progression. Some are highly evolved, and others are much less so. Some have had physical lives on the earth and are in between lifetimes. Others have "graduated" and do not have to return unless they choose, in order to help mankind. Still others have not incarnated in our physical world, helping us from the other side.

Whether we call them spirits or angels or guides does not matter. There is considerable anecdotal evidence that they exist, and this evidence has been gathered from many diverse cultures and religions over many centuries.

Babies and young children are often aware of the loving spirits or energies around us, but their communication skills are limited. We adults tend not to believe them, relegating their observations and perceptions to the realm of imagination and fantasy. Yet what they are aware of is often very real.

When we die and leave our physical bodies, we proceed to that level of consciousness at which we are most comfortable. The more loving and wise we are, the more advanced we will be on the other side.

I am still amazed by the similarity of the knowledge my patients transmit to me while they are in deep meditative or hypnotic states. High school dropouts, nuclear physicists, attorneys, and professional athletes alike tell me virtually the same things about the spiritual state and our purpose on this earth. This lends considerable credence to their experiences.

Once more I want to emphasize that these findings are clinical, accumulated from many hundreds of patients. Finding so much similarity and so many correlations is highly significant statistically.

Certain individuals are more adept at communicating knowledge from spiritual sources. The late American psychic Edgar Cayce is one example, and his work has been carefully studied and analyzed. We all know about the skills of some of the seers and clairvoyants of the East, such as Paramahansa Yogananda, but people with similar abilities also exist in the

Western world. I have been blessed to meet with a few of them, and I have been doubly blessed to discover that their work validates the experiences and accounts of my patients.

I evaluate my experiences with the trained mind of a psychiatrist. Being analytical is completely compatible with being open-minded. I have met people with amazing abilities, and I have met those whose skills are limited or non-existent.

Spirits, as well as people, are of many levels. Those of the lower levels can transmit misleading or even harmful messages, usually to people with limited mediumistic ability or lack of proper spiritual development. Spirits of higher levels seem to be accessible only to those people with higher spiritual development and/or those with proper intent, those without ulterior motives for self-gain at the expense of others.

When you meet a seer or wise teacher whose motive is to help others to understand, to heal other people's hearts and to assist them on their spiritual path, a profound shift in your consciousness can occur. The world will seem different, filled with unseen helpers and bathed in a loving energy that refreshes and renews your soul.

You yourself may spontaneously experience other life-transforming events. Dreams, déjà vu experiences, clairvoyant episodes, and other paranormal occurrences (including NDEs) can induce a permanent awakening to the true nature of reality. Meditation can increase the likelihood that one or more of these experiences may happen.

But we humans tend to forget, or at least to rationalize and minimize, any experience we consider "improbable" or "extraordinary." Moreover, we allow our "logical" minds to subtract the spiritual meaning from the experience. Someone once said that what we call coincidences are really God's fingerprints.

I cannot regress enough of you, nor can I train enough therapists to treat everyone (in the world). I can, however, share these true stories and experiences with you, reminding you once again about your spiritual nature and about the abundant loving and helping energy that fills and surrounds you at all times.

As the Christian mystics taught, you are not a human being having a spiritual experience. You are a *spiritual* being having a human experience.

As I have explored more and more of the human mind and the limits of consciousness, I have come across some people with extraordinary abilities. Some can access information not normally available through the five senses. They seem to possess a sixth sense, an inner knowing or intuition, and sometimes the information received in this manner can be quite accurate.

Others have mediumistic abilities, the capacity to receive and to transmit messages and knowledge from beings "on the other side," whether from spirit guides, from loved ones who have died, or from other sources of consciousness outside the usual limits of the body and the brain.

People who are truly gifted need not cheat, use tricks or magic. They know things they "cannot" know under our present conceptions of how human minds operate. Their abilities are real.

On the other hand, the field of psychics and mediums is filled with opportunists, fakes, and manipulators. It is very important to be able to separate the real ones from the fakes.

Here are some rules of thumb:

1. We are all psychic and possess intuitive abilities far beyond what we know or use. Carefully weigh any information or material you receive from a psychic on the scales of your own intuitive wisdom. If the information given to you does not feel right or does not fit, it probably is incorrect. You are psychic too.

2. All the information received by psychics or mediums is necessarily processed by the medium before it can be transmitted to you. Therefore the information can be significantly distorted by the psychic's mental processes. The amount of distortion depends on the medium's individual agenda. Psychics are human, so even a gifted psychic can deliver distorted information if his or her personal problems, moods, concerns, or desires interfere with the psychic process.

3. Opportunists usually charge a lot of money, attempt to make you dependent on their advice, and set themselves up as "special," with abilities no one else possesses, or as gurus you must follow. Try to exit quickly when you become aware of these tactics.

   I was amazed to find that in South America gifted mediums and healers, many of whom make their living in other professions, will often travel to the home of a financially needy person who needs help or healing. They take time off from their work, pay for their own transportation, and charge their clients nothing. Several of these visits may occur over a one- or two-week interval.

4. True growth is an inner process. While a psychic can help you learn to access your inner wisdom, with enough meditation, you become your own psychic and transcend the need for external guidance. In the beginning, however, the validation from a psychic or medium functioning with a minimal amount of distortion can be very helpful.

5. Psychic and mediumistic abilities are not necessarily correlated with spiritual evolution. Some very gifted mediums have been known to behave quite selfishly, even despicably. Don't confer unwarranted spiritual status on someone merely because he or she possesses extraordinary paranormal abilities. You set yourself up to be manipulated and

victimized when you believe that because a medium is talented, he or she is necessarily an ethical person.

6. It is also wise to remember that for the most part, mediums and psychics are not therapists or mental health counselors trained in therapeutic techniques. Do not expect your fears, symptoms, or problems to disappear miraculously in the wake of a session with a psychic. Do not anticipate a therapeutic interpretation that will suddenly tie all your issues together and provide a healing understanding. This is not what they do. Lacking years of training, most are not prepared to analyze and interpret the material that may arise. They discern it, and they present it to you. You may receive a glimpse into another world, and this glimpse may be extremely valuable and healing to you, but such a glimpse is not psychotherapy.

   If a medium tells you something inaccurate or even hurtful, remember that he or she is not necessarily a wise and compassionate therapist. Judge the medium, if you must, the same as you would any other person. Do not surrender your power or integrity to anyone.

7. While we often admire, and even envy, people with advanced psychic or mediumistic abilities, we should not lose sight of our real goals. We are here to learn and to grow as spiritual beings, to become more loving and more compassionate, to achieve a balance and harmony in our lives, to feel and maintain a solid sense of inner peace. We are not here, again with some few exceptions, to become famous psychics. Psychic and mediumistic talents may increase as we progress along the spiritual path, but they are not the goal. They line the path, they shed some light on the trail, but they are not an end in themselves.

   Years ago I heard a story about Buddha and his disciples. One day, they were meditating in a quiet garden when one of the disciples, deep in a meditative state, began to levitate. Feeling his body lifting itself up from the ground, he became very excited, and very proud of his accomplishment. He stirred himself from his meditation and felt himself back on the ground. He stood up and walked over to Buddha.

"I have mastered levitation," the disciple announced.

"That's nice," Buddha responded, "but don't let it distract you from your meditation."

8. Some gifted people appear to be able to communicate with spirits on the other side. However we may interpret the possible methods and mechanisms, something very real and powerful is happening. Because someone has died and returned to spiritual form does not immediately confer great wisdom to this being. The same is true for spiritual guides and guardians. There exists a hierarchy of levels, from ignorant and foolish spirits to those who are truly advanced masters. Obviously it is important to discern the differences. If someone is channeling a foolish and ignorant spirit, why in the world should you listen to what is being said?

How do you know? Again, use your own intuitional wisdom. You can recognize higher-level spirits by the loving content as well as the accuracy of their messages. They often have access to private details that validate the experience.

9. The medium may receive messages from the other side in the form of symbols, metaphors, or visions. This part of the communication might be very accurate. However, in an attempt to interpret or make sense of the symbol, the medium often introduces distortion to the message. The medium's interpretation could be misleading or inaccurate. For example, the medium might become aware of a rose and ask if the client has a garden or if flowers are important to the client. The client may become confused. In ac-

tuality, the image could be a reference to the client's deceased grandmother whose name was Rose. Ideally, the medium should merely describe what he or she sees: "Does 'rose' mean something to you?"

Sometimes, particularly when the messages received are in the form of words, the medium may find the communication unclear, as if he or she were listening to a radio with heavy static. Words can be misinterpreted under these conditions. This "interference" explains why mediums are often asking the spirits with whom they are in contact for a yes-or-no answer to their questions. The answers tell them whether they are accurately reading or interpreting the signals being received.

10. Gifted psychics and mediums can help us enormously, especially when they provide glimpses of the other side and bring us messages from our departed loved ones. Through them we experience the reality of life after death, the nature of our immortal souls, the opportunities for being reunited with our families and friends. They can provide guidance about how to live our lives, about values, about what is important and what is not. But ultimately, we need to experience these things directly, within ourselves. When we experience, then we really know. When we can hear or see or sense our deceased loved ones directly, then we know we are separated only in a temporary way. When we can, with ecstasy and wonder, directly experience the divine, we awaken like the sages and mystics before us.

There are many ways to increase your own psychic sensitivities. Listen to and trust your intuitions. Observe how often you are correct. For example, when the phone rings, guess who is calling. The first name or thought that pops into your awareness is often the most accurate. Practice similar intuitional games whenever you have the opportunity (i.e., what color will your friend be wearing when you meet later). Many of the exercises you will find later in this book, such as psychometry, "Faces," energy scanning, and visualizations, will also allow you to further practice and refine your own psychic and intuitive abilities. Mediumistic skills also may emerge when you work with these exercises. The two longer meditations in Appendix B will provide powerful practice as well.

The art of meditation is also discussed in more detail later. The regular practice of meditation or related introspective techniques also opens psychic channels and allows you to experience the psycho-spiritual world directly.

Your intention to open yourself to psychic and mediumistic experiences is also important. Before going to sleep, instruct yourself to be receptive to psychic dreams and messages. Ask for them to occur and remember to journal your experiences upon awakening.

Even the growing awareness that your real nature is spiritual will increase the likelihood of having mystical and psychic experiences. Your mind will become more comfortable and familiar with such phenomena, encouraging even more events to happen. As the writer Wayne Dyer has said, "You will see it when you believe it."

A patient of mine was grieving deeply over the death of her son. He had died in 1994 at the age of thirteen. His death was sudden and unexpected, due to an undiagnosed enlargement of his heart. His sister was with him when he died.

The family started to see me to help cope with their tragedy. Now two years later, the mother came to the office with her husband, her twelve-year-old daughter, and her infant daughter, who was hungry and fidgeting. She went off with the baby to breast-feed while the other two waited with me in my office.

We began talking about driving, and the father suddenly looked very sad.

"What is wrong?" I asked.

"My son would have been fifteen now. I would be teaching him to drive, if he were alive. . . . I've always looked forward to driving with him, and now I will never have the opportunity," he said quietly.

We discussed his sadness for a while, and then moved on to other subjects.

When mother and baby returned, I began a guided imagery exercise with the mother and older daughter. Father was walking the baby to sleep in the back of my office. I instructed the two participants to visualize a beautiful treasure chest and to fill this chest with those things they really need in their lives. Quietly, the mother began to weep.

Later on, I asked her what she had experienced.

"I saw my son," she replied, "and he was very vivid and real to me. I started to put him into the treasure chest, and then he spoke to me!"

"You don't have to put me into that treasure chest," he said.

"But I want you with me all the time," she had answered.

"I am with you all the time," he responded. "I love you all. . . . Tell Daddy he's right. I love to drive with him, especially when he's by himself."

She had not known about her husband's sadness and regret or our earlier conversation. Her powerful vision and conversation with her son helped her greatly in beginning to heal her grief. This was her *own* experience, and she received immediate validation from her husband and older daughter. She had made a contact with her son. She felt that she had indeed talked to him. Her family bonded around this direct experience with him. They still grieved, but their recovery had started.

We are all spiritual beings. We are all capable of having direct psychic and mediumistic experiences, just as this grieving mother did with her son.

Yet, for the majority of us, it is easier to receive such messages from the other side in a slightly more indirect way, from the gifted medium whose heart is in the right place. The impact of these messages from our deceased loved ones can still be extremely powerful and life-transforming.

CHAPTER THIRTEEN

Extraordinary Messages

It is on this Plane that some souls are allowed to manifest themselves to the people who are still in physical form. They are allowed to come back. . . . On this plane intercommunication is allowed. This is where you're allowed to use your psychic abilities and communicate with people in physical form. There are many ways to do this. Some are allowed the power of sight and can show themselves to the people still in physical form. Others have the power of movement and are allowed to move objects telepathically. Many people choose to come here because they are allowed to see those who are still in physical form and very close to them.

The gifted psychic and medium Char gave a reading to my teenage daughter, Amy. The day before, Carole and I had attended the funeral of the grandfather of Amy's good friend, David. Amy knew this man as Buzzy, his nickname.

"I have a message for someone named David," Char told her. "It's from his grandfather, whose name is Howard . . . or Harold," she went on with uncanny accuracy. Amy had never known that Buzzy's name was Howard.

"Tell them that he loves them and he's fine. He's with Max and Sam."

None of us knew Max or Sam. The next day we learned that Sam was Buzzy's father and Max was Sam's good friend and business partner for twenty-five years.

We do not die when our physical bodies die. A part of us goes on. Spirit, soul, consciousness. It is like walking through a door into another room, a larger, brighter, wonderful room.

This is why we should not be afraid. We are always surrounded by love. Our loved ones never leave. We are all beautiful and immortal souls. We are in our bodies for a while, but we are not our bodies.

When my patients and others receive messages from loved ones who have died, the messages are amazingly similar. Whether in regressions, in dreams, from mediums, or in any other way, there is a common theme.

"I love you. I am fine. Take care of yourself and do not grieve so much for me."

They are always telling us not to mourn. They know something we have forgotten.

They are immortal, and so are we.

One of the most powerful experiences of my life occurred when I received an extraordinary message during a regression with Catherine. I share this story so you may understand a moment that forever changed my life.

The greatest tragedy in my life had been the unexpected death of our firstborn son, Adam, who was only twenty-three days old when he died, early in 1971. About ten days after we had brought him home from the hospital, he had developed respiratory problems and projectile vomiting. The diagnosis was extremely difficult to make. "Total anomalous pulmonary venous drainage with an atrial septal defect," we were told. "It occurs once in approximately every ten million births." The pulmonary veins, which were supposed to bring oxygenated blood back to the heart, were incorrectly routed, entering the heart on the wrong side. It was as if his heart were turned around, backward. Extremely, extremely rare.

Heroic open-heart surgery could not save Adam, who died several days later. We mourned for months, our hopes and dreams dashed. Our son Jordan was born a year later, a balm for our wounds.

At the time of Adam's death, I had been wavering about my earlier choice of psychiatry as a career. I was enjoying my internship in internal medicine, and I had been offered a residency position in medicine. After Adam's death, I firmly decided that I would make psychiatry my profession. I was angry that modern medicine, with all of its advanced skills and technology, could not save my son, this simple, tiny baby.

My father had been in excellent health until he experienced a massive heart attack early in 1979, at the age of sixty-one. He survived the initial attack, but his heart wall had been irretrievably damaged, and he died three days later. This was about nine months before Catherine's first appointment.

My father had been a religious man, more ritualistic than spiritual. His Hebrew name, Avrom, suited him better than the English, Alvin. Four months after his death, our daughter, Amy, was born, and she was named after him.

Here, in 1982, in my quiet, darkened office, a deafening cascade of hidden, secret truths was pouring upon me. I was swimming in a spiritual sea, and I loved the water. My arms were gooseflesh. Catherine could not possibly know this information. There was no place even to look it up. My father's Hebrew name, that I had a son who died in infancy from a one-in-ten-million heart defect, my brooding about medicine, my father's death, and my daughter's naming—it was too much, too specific, too true. This unsophisticated laboratory technician was a conduit for transcendental knowledge. And if she could reveal these truths, what else was there? I needed to know more.

"Who," I sputtered, "who is there? Who tells you these things?"

"The Masters," she whispered. "The Master Spirits tell me. They tell me I have lived eighty-six times in physical state."

Catherine's breathing slowed, and her head stopped rolling from side to side. She was resting. I wanted to go on, but the implications of what she had said were distracting me. Did she really have eighty-six previous lifetimes? And what about "the Masters"? Could it be? Could our lives be guided by spirits?

The message regarding my father and my son opened my mind to the possibility of eternity and paranormal phenomena. After this and the subsequent experiences with other patients, my values began to shift toward the spiritual and away from the material, more toward people and relationships and less toward accumulating things. I became more aware of what we take with us and what we don't. Indeed, before these experiences, I did not even believe that a part of us survived physical death.

In my travels through Brazil, a spiritually progressed country, I have met many talented and enlightened people. I was very impressed by a medium named Celia.

A friend of mine impulsively took me to a group session Celia was conducting in a working-class area of Rio de Janeiro. Celia knew nothing about me or my books. She spoke only Portuguese, so my friend translated for me.

I was sitting near the front of the auditorium. People had written names on pieces of paper and then put them in a basket. Celia took these pieces, crumpled them, and, without looking, called out certain names. People, recognizing the names of their deceased loved ones, approached the small raised podium where Celia was sitting. Sometimes individuals or couples would come up, sometimes entire families.

The emotion on their faces, reflected in their body language, was genuine and spontaneous. More than eight hundred people from all social classes were in the audience. Nobody knew if or when he or she would be called up.

I have rarely seen anyone work as rapidly as Celia. A torrent of exact names, descriptions of physical characteristics and personality traits all poured forth like a waterfall of facts. Not only did she know how people died, she had access to private and confidential details from the deceased person's life, details the families found enormously comforting. Her words emerged with a force that belied her small, frail sixty-five- or seventy-year-old body. She was shorter than five feet tall, and she needed an inhaler to keep her asthma in check.

Two stories were extraordinarily touching. Celia called out a man's name and his mother, father, and sister came up to the podium. I saw that the family was shaking as Celia vividly described the terrible automobile accident in which the young man had been killed. She told them that he was fine now and sending his love, but that he was not alone. Two other young people had died with him in that car. Celia called out two more names and, in a surreal tableau, the grieving families of the other two victims approached the podium. The father of one of these children stood in back of the others, holding himself stiffly erect and a bit separate, obviously struggling to control his emotions. The others were weeping and holding onto each other.

Celia turned to the aloof man's wife. "Do not feel so guilty. They are all well now, in spirit." This woman's son had been the driver of the car, apparently responsible for the accident, and the mother had been feeling particularly terrible.

"They send you their love," Celia continued, and she added many more personal details.

Then she took a long look at the man who was standing stiffly behind the others. She stood, and even though she was standing on the podium behind a small table and the others were shakily standing on the floor, her head was still not much higher than the others. She wanted to see him even more clearly.

"Your son tells me that you are having a harder time accepting all of this, that it is more difficult for you because you are an engineer." The man nodded at the accuracy of these comments.

"He says that you can stop arguing about the carpet. It is unimportant now."

At this comment, the father broke down. Hugging his wife, he began to cry. Unbeknownst to the others, he and his wife had been arguing about a particular carpet in their house for some time. The father insisted the dust of this carpet was responsible for his son's allergies and asthmatic attacks. His wife, however, was convinced her beloved carpet was blameless, and refused to part with it.

The extremely personal nature of this comment broke through the engineer's intellect and touched his heart. He could no longer deny what he was experiencing. He held his wife tightly as they sobbed together, knowing their son was still alive in spirit, knowing that we are not our bodies, and we never really die.

After a few other emotional and accurate communications from the other side, Celia called the name of a man who had been shot and murdered three weeks previously. The wife of the slain man and his two physician sons walked to the podium.

The messages Celia delivered were filled with private details. Then she described the shooting and the medical treatments that followed. She used highly technical medical terms, even wandering into the intricacies of quantum physics. I doubted that Celia had special training in medicine or physics, and my translator confirmed this.

As the dead man conveyed his love for his family, the three hugged each other tightly. The healing they were experiencing was palpable throughout the room.

Celia was not finished, however. She had a beautiful spiritual message to deliver.

"He appreciates your sympathy and your love, but he wants you to also feel sympathy for the man who shot him. Let go of your anger. This man is of a lower level and does not yet understand spiritual laws. He will pay a heavy price for his actions, yet because he is ignorant, he needs help. He needs your prayers. He did not understand; therefore he should not be judged."

After sixty or seventy readings, Celia took a break. I was led to a small room with about a dozen other people. Celia was already resting in a chair, and I was introduced to her as a famous doctor from America who wrote and lectured about reincarnation and other spiritual matters. From the questions she asked about my work, it was evident that Celia was not familiar with me or my works. Then she blessed my work, and I praised her abilities. We agreed that only unconditional love really matters.

Suddenly and without any real change in her voice or tone, she started giving *me* messages.

"Your son Adam is here, and he wants you to know that his heart is now in the correct position. He watches over and protects his brother, Jordan, and his sister, with the same name as the father. He sends his love to his mother, Carole. [She pronounced the name Ca-ró-lee.] His death was important to bring you peace and serenity later, through your work."

Carole's father and her uncle, both of whom died many years ago, were the only people who pronounced her name that way. It was their pet name for her.

Celia's voice now changed tone a bit, and she became more serious.

"Your spiritual work is exactly right; it is correct and good. Don't get discouraged . . . continue. The work is helping everywhere, even on the other side. It will grow even larger."

As Celia's words entered my mind and my heart, I remembered Catherine's messages seventeen years earlier, moving and life-changing messages from my father and my son Adam. A chill came over me, these seventeen years later.

I knew that Celia knew nothing about me or my family and that she had not read my books. Her accuracy gave me goose bumps.

After all these years, I still don't take "miracles" for granted.

Celia did not know that I do get discouraged from time to time because the demands of the work keep me from family and friends, because I cannot possibly respond to the many requests for help, and because of the relentless onslaught from skeptics and critics. Celia's words revived my heart and refreshed my soul.

The eight hundred people and I were sharing a remarkable experience. As I returned to the larger room, I felt the peaceful, loving energy that filled the building. I talked briefly to the four families whose messages I described above. None had ever met or talked to Celia or her staff before the moment they were called.

The next morning I phoned my friend to thank him for taking me to Celia. He said that he had spoken to Celia after I had left, and she had told him that many more spirits were there for me when I was in the room with her. Many were trying to come through with messages for me, but she did not want to overload or overwhelm me. And so she stopped with Adam's message. A brief wave of disappointment washed over me. I wanted to hear and experience much more. But I was happy with what I had observed and heard throughout that day. And my discouragement faded.

A few years earlier, James Van Praagh, the American medium and author of the international best-seller *Talking to Heaven* and now *Reaching to Heaven,* had predicted that my work would be reaching larger and larger audiences. He told me that I was in a transition period to an even higher level of influence in the world, which desperately needed a spiritual direction and a melding of science and spirituality.

My mind heard these predictions, but I didn't really believe them. There just seemed to be too much opposition and skepticism in the way. For nine years I had been exhausting myself trying to teach about the truth and reality of life after death, reincarnation, and divine love. For nine years I had been ridiculed and mocked for teaching that love never stops, that we and our loved ones do not die when our bodies die, that we continue to exist and continue to love as spirits and, if necessary, back here in physical state. I knew I was teaching the truth, but so many people keep their minds closed. How could the work reach a higher level, and why now?

During and shortly after the Brazil trip, three things happened that, in sequence, began to awaken me and to alert me to the possibility that Celia and James were correct.

The first was the size of the crowds and the media reaction to my talks and workshops in Brazil. In every city I visited, thousands of people poured into the auditoriums. Every event was sold out. Television, newspapers, and magazines covered all events. Book signings would go on for hours because of the huge number of people waiting patiently in the long lines.

Yet my mind managed to discount this huge reaction. "This is Brazil," I rationalized. Brazil is a country of immense spiritual awareness and enlightenment, a land of spectacular physical beauty but especially of beautiful people. The people are open-minded, loving, and already spiritually awakened. Spiritists such as Allan Kardec have already paved the way.

Brazil is an exception, I thought, as are many of the other countries of Latin America, where people feel free to talk about and share their spiritual experiences.

Then the second event occurred. Over the years I have treated many celebrities, political leaders, sports stars, and others in my practice. Many have had dramatic experiences, whether of past lives or of other spiritual phenomena. Because of the rules of confidentiality and respect for their privacy, I cannot talk or write about them. They, of course, are not bound by the same restrictions. Yet, because of their concern about public reaction, it is very rare for someone of their prominence to talk about me, my books, or our work together.

One exception has been Gloria Estefan. An incredibly talented singer and actress who is also a person of enormous physical and moral courage, she is very advanced spiritually. Gloria has a beautiful heart and has helped the Miami community in numerous charitable ways. So when she went public about me, I was thrilled but not surprised.

In a magazine article in June 1996, Gloria said, "I have meditated my whole life, almost as a form of self-hypnosis, but I didn't really know what it was until after my tour bus accident, when a friend of mine sent me the book *Many Lives, Many Masters* by Brian Weiss. It made a big impact on me and gave me a lot of strength during my recovery. I drew upon it often. I was always curious about hypnosis without realizing that I'd been doing a form of it myself for years. Eventually, I met Brian Weiss, and when he hypnotized me, he used the same method that I have been using since I was a child to do a kind of inner meditation. That has been my way of praying as well."

But Gloria was not the second event. Sylvester Stallone was.

While I was in Brazil in August of 1997, he told the American press about how I helped him prepare for his role in *Cop Land,* his new movie.

Critics were praising Stallone's acting in *Cop Land.* He was not playing an action hero again, but a much more dramatically demanding role as a physically impaired sheriff fighting corruption in a small town.

The newspapers wrote: "Stallone underwent internal preparation as well—especially knowing he'd be working opposite [Robert] De Niro, [Harvey] Keitel and Ray Liotta.

" 'I had never worked with such good actors before,' he says, confessing some trepidation, 'and suddenly I was thrown into this arena that was like going from the Cub Scouts to the Green Berets!'

"One of the things he did was to consult Dr. Brian Weiss, author of the best-selling *Many Lives, Many Masters.* Weiss, a Miami psychiatrist who mixes hypnosis, spiritual psychotherapy and past life regression into his practice, helped Stallone tap into something he'd forgotten.

" '[Weiss] came upon the idea of nonphysical courage, which is the bravest of all: A man who enters a situation knowing there's no chance he can physically survive the outcome, but he willingly does it for an ideal,' Stallone says.

"Weiss says his meeting with Stallone wasn't about unearthing any past lives. 'It was not a doctor-patient thing. This character was a hero of a deeper moral and spiritual courage, and he was concerned about being able to express that. My impression was that Stallone has these qualities innately; all I did was help him remove any possible obstacles to his expression of these qualities.'

"Such extensive preparation for a movie was something Stallone hadn't done in a very long time—not because he hadn't wanted to, but because the roles he was taking didn't require much more from him other than to show up, dodge bullets, and hang from an occasional mountain."

The fact that Sylvester Stallone had the courage to mention me publicly meant that millions more people became aware of the work.

The third event happened only a few days after Sylvester Stallone's quote and Celia's messages. This event had a great impact on me personally, but it was much more private.

I had returned to Miami from Brazil on August 19, 1997. On August 22, I received a phone call in my office. The phone call was from Kensington Palace in London, the home of Diana, Princess of Wales. Princess Diana's personal assistant, Jacqueline Allen, was on the line.

"The Princess loved your book *Only Love Is Real*," Jacqueline told me. "It brought her great comfort and peace. She would like to talk with you. Are you planning a trip to England in the near future?"

"No," I answered. "There is nothing scheduled, but I am sure we can arrange something."

"Well, she is on holiday now. She would like to contact you when she returns to England."

"That would be my pleasure," I responded. "I'm going to send her my other books and some audiotapes."

We sent her a package of books and tapes that afternoon, and I looked forward to her call. I had admired her courage, her compassion, and her charitable work, and the way she seemed able to show great love to people with AIDS and other afflictions.

Of course, Princess Diana never did call me. On August 31, just before she was to return to England, she and Dodi Fayed were killed in that terrible automobile crash in a tunnel in Paris.

I do not believe in coincidences, and I am writing this section about Princess Diana now only a few days after her death.

I am deeply saddened although I know she is fine, that her loving and shining soul is alive and well and clothed in light and in love on the other side. Still, there is always a sorrow when people leave us physically.

I believe there are two reasons why I heard from Kensington Palace the week before Princess Diana's death.

Only Love Is Real is a book about soulmates and about love. It is about people who have that special connection that transcends time and space. It is about people who have been together before, in past lifetimes or across spiritual dimensions, and who find their loved ones again, in this life. They learn that love is eternal and absolute. Love never ends, not even by death. We are always loved. We are never alone. We are always reunited with our loved ones.

I believe that Princess Diana felt a soulmate connection to Dodi Fayed, and probably to her sons and to other loved ones as well. Perhaps *Only Love Is Real* helped her to understand these powerful connections.

The other reason is that people often have premonitions or strong intuitive feelings about important events in their lives. Frequently these feelings are about impending deaths, whether theirs or of other people close to them. There are so many accounts of people saying good-bye in one way or another just before their unexpected death.

One of my patients, the young pregnant wife of a businessman killed in an airplane crash in Colombia, had recurrent dreams of his death in a plane crash for the entire month before it happened. How could she have been warned in advance if this were truly a random accident?

Another patient was a woman in Miami whose brother was killed in a car accident in Michigan. Weeks *before* the accident she had visited funeral homes to get more information. Perhaps Diana knew, at some level.

Only Love Is Real, just like *Many Lives, Many Masters* and

Through Time Into Healing, is not only about soulmates and past lives. It is about truth and divine love. It explains that there really is no death, only life; that our souls are eternal and can never be harmed; that we will always meet our loved ones again, in spirit and in body. These are books of hope, not just because they are comforting, but because they are true. Perhaps the book comforted Princess Diana about the earlier death of her beloved father. Was she still grieving for him? Was her "comfort and peace" related to him?

Princess Diana read my book just before her death. The timing is not a coincidence. She learned more about soulmates, but she also learned more about souls. I am sure her reception on the other side was resplendent with brilliant light, loving greetings, and incredible joy.

I will miss her. I hope my book was able to help her a little bit.

The small conference room was packed with one hundred fifty people hanging on his every word as I witnessed the spiritual medium James Van Praagh convey information from deceased loved ones. Even the skeptics among us had to marvel at the small evidential details he delivered to those hungry for proof that their loved ones lived on. Those he addressed acknowledged his accuracy. The more intimate the detail, the more astonished, and the more touched, we all were.

Carole and I were sitting about halfway back in the audience. I was having trouble intellectually understanding how James could know these small facts. "They tell me," is always his simple answer.

On my left sat a woman who looked to be in her mid-thirties. James called out a man's name, and an older woman on the other side of her shakily rose from her chair. "That's my mother," the younger woman confided to me.

A stream of confirming details, which some call "evidentials," flew from James to the older woman, who was in her sixties. "Yes . . . yes . . . oh, yes!" she kept replying. Her hands were tensed into tight balls. Her legs were unsteady.

"He thanks you for tending to his roses," James went on. "He knows you do this because of your love for him, and he returns love to you." The older woman nodded, tears falling from her eyes.

"And don't worry about the dogs," James said enigmatically, with a touch of humor.

Her daughter turned to me to explain. "She *does* tend to my father's rose garden; she seems driven to do so . . . and she worries so about our dogs running through and ruining the garden . . . this is so amazing!" Her eyes were also welling with tears. I was so touched by what was happening that I had to struggle to maintain some objectivity and distance.

Soon James had everyone crying.

"He thanks you for bringing something of his here today. . . ." James paused for a moment. "It's a ring, he's telling me. It's his ring, and you've brought it with you to help his chances of coming through."

As James finished, the woman slowly stretched out her arm in front of her and opened her left hand, which throughout the reading had been tightly clenched. In her hand was her husband's ring, which even I, two seats away, had not noticed until that moment. All in the room were deeply moved. A glowing smile spread across the older woman's face. She *knew* her husband was there communicating with her.

"She never carries around that ring," her daughter answered to my inquiring look. "She only brought it to this conference hoping that it would help. . . . I guess it did," she added, tears rolling gently down her cheeks.

Mediums are not mind readers. Wherever their inspiration or knowledge derives, it is not from the minds of their clients or audiences. Another James Van Praagh vignette illustrates this point.

Working with an audience of nearly six hundred people in the ballroom of a hotel in Fort Lauderdale, Florida, James was once again "directed" to specific people in the audience. I had just observed him helping a grieving couple whose seven-year-old daughter had recently died of leukemia.

"She sends her love and is very grateful to you for keeping her with all the toys and dolls and the unicorns."

Although this made no sense at that moment to me, the young parents reacted immediately. With great emotion, they explained that their daughter had been cremated. The box with her ashes was kept in her bedroom, among the young girl's dolls and toys. The bedsheets and pillowcases were their daughter's favorite ones, decorated with unicorns.

James had never met or talked with these young parents before that moment. Neither did he realize that the next person to whom he was directed was a young woman whom I knew. James had just arrived from California, where he lives, and had not met her before.

"I have David here . . . David . . . somebody's son, who has died and is in spirit," James began.

A few women stood up, as David is not a rare name. But the young woman I know did not stand. She has no children. Her husband's brother, whose name was David, had died suddenly two years previously, but thus far the information was not specific enough for her to respond.

James did not seem to connect with any of the women who had responded.

"Who's the pilot?" James then asked. "He's telling me about a pilot. Someone with David who is a pilot."

Now the women who were standing sat down, but the young woman shakily stood.

"I have a David," she said. "He is my brother-in-law, my

husband's brother. And he died two years ago. His mother is a pilot. . . . She flies airplanes."

Now James seemed satisfied that the proper connection had been made.

"He wants to give his love to her," James added. Then he looked up and to the side, as if he were listening to someone. When he looked back to the young woman, he looked up, above her head.

"I see a red knife over your head," he told her. "I'm being shown that somebody . . . has been looking at this knife and thinking about cleaning the knife."

The young woman knew nothing about a red knife. Neither she nor her husband owned one. She could not confirm this information.

"Keep it," James added, meaning to remember this for the future. Then he moved on to the next "stranger," because everyone in the ballroom was new to him.

A few days later I talked to the young woman. "You won't believe this," she told me.

When she returned home after the workshop concluded, she had called her mother-in-law, who lives in rural Pennsylvania. She did not tell her mother-in-law, David's mother, about the workshop or about James. She merely asked one question.

"Does a red knife mean anything to you?"

"It's funny you should ask that," her mother-in-law responded. "Yesterday [the day before the workshop], I was down in the basement cleaning up and moving some fishing equipment. I saw David's old Swiss Army knife, and I picked it up. I remember thinking, I really should clean this knife."

James had become aware of a thought in the mind of David's mother, who had picked up the red knife and experienced the thought about cleaning it the day *before* the workshop. The young woman in the audience had no knowledge of this knife or of the thought, which occurred in the basement of a house more than one thousand miles distant.

The details of Swiss Army knives, pilots, unicorns, and so on are much too specific to be relegated to the categories of coincidence or generality.

We can all learn to do what James does, as you will see throughout this book, but we lack the confidence and the practice to realize this. I like to use the analogy of playing the piano when I talk about learning to use our psychic abilities. Not everyone is born with the talent to be a virtuoso pianist. However, with lessons and with practice and hard work, all of us can learn to bang out a few tunes. The same is true with developing our intuitive processes.

Eventually we will understand that all wisdom is within us, and as we remember, practice, and access this wisdom, we will become our own best teacher. At this point, we will find peace and joy in the present time, because the real issue is about how we live our lives right now, being spiritual *now*, no matter what we have been taught to believe.

And as we awaken, the spirits will sing their love songs directly to our ears.

Sitting more or less anonymously in the audience of the *Maury Povich* show in late August of 1997, I watched the renowned British healer and medium Rosemary Altea give intimate and specific details to a panel of people who were grief-stricken from the tragic loss of their loved ones. Carole and I had been visiting in New York City, and we had stopped by to say hello to Joni Evans, my literary agent, the day before the taping. Joni is also Rosemary's agent, and she impulsively invited us to sit in the audience for the show. Rosemary did not know we would be there.

Like Celia and James Van Praagh, Rosemary, the author of *The Eagle and the Rose* and *Proud Spirit,* is exceedingly adept at relaying messages from the other side. In order to use her gifts to better the world, she has founded the Rosemary Altea Association of Healers, RAAH, a non-profit organization based in England. Although I have enjoyed her books and had watched her before on television, this was my first chance to watch Rosemary work in person. There are so few psychics and mediums who are really good and accurate in their work that I jumped at this opportunity.

Unfortunately, on American television everything has to be a test. Rosemary was supposed to provide precise details about the dead loved ones of people she was meeting for the first time and about whose lives she knew nothing. All this on television in front of a live studio audience.

Talk about pressure, I thought. She should be meeting with them privately and without any of these distractions. Still, Rosemary seemed okay with the arrangement. And I understood that television thrives on capturing people's spontaneous reactions. In my mind I wished her well despite the obstacles, knowing that this was not a fair scientific evaluation of her abilities.

Rosemary overcame all these impediments and, with amazing accuracy, provided fact after fact to the grieving families. The comfort, hope, and relief she provided were palpable to all. The entire audience shared in this moving and dramatic experience.

Unknown to everyone, I already knew two of the people on the stage with Rosemary. Ralph and Kathy Robinson had attended one of my conferences a year previously, and we had spent considerable time talking about the tragic death of their young son, Ryan, who had been accidentally shot by a friend.

Ryan and his friend were at an unsupervised teenage party when they found a Russian handgun. They believed that the gun was not loaded, because the safety on this particular gun allowed the trigger to be pulled back and clicked. They had pulled the trigger many times with no bullet ever firing. But somehow the safety accidentally was switched off. There was a lone bullet in the chamber, and on a cold October evening shortly after his sixteenth birthday, Ryan died of a gunshot wound to his head.

The Robinsons' world fell apart. They were consumed with grief.

I knew the details of Ryan's death and many of the details of his short life. Rosemary, not knowing any of this, turned to them. "Bang!" she said loudly. "He keeps saying 'Bang!'" She even described the smell surrounding this horrible accident, and she added many more details.

Ryan's parents, both of whom are sophisticated people, were visibly moved. I knew the encounter with Rosemary would help them heal even beyond what I could do for them.

"He's so cheeky," Rosemary added, accurately describing Ryan but temporarily confusing his mother. "Cheeky" is a term used in Britain to describe healthily impish, mischievous personalities, and Ryan certainly fit the bill. Once explained, his mother heartily nodded her agreement.

A few days later, Ralph wrote me a letter:

"Well, either the production crew was feeding Rosemary information about our loss of Ryan or she is nothing short of phenomenal. She was so gracious in her relationship with us. She came into the holding room before the show to connect with each of us and tell us how she worked. After the show she again spent time with our group to make sure everyone felt complete. . . . All in all, it was a very rewarding experience and we were both very glad that we had participated."

Ryan's death and their experiences afterwards have brought enormous spiritual growth to the Robinsons, who have been developing projects to help Compassionate Friends, a national organization that provides support to bereaved families.

To me, there are no coincidences. The Robinsons have been giving profusely to others, and now Rosemary could give something back to them. And I, a kind of common denominator, could witness the whole process.

With his letter, Ralph included a poem written by his son. "We didn't know he wrote any poetry until we discovered his journals after he was gone."

Follow the Wind

Follow the wind
To *other* sides
That call for you.

Can you capture
The life that has
yet to be lived?

That stained soul
Can be cleaned
With time and faith.

—by Ryan J. Robinson

In another letter, Ralph wrote, "I have learned how important it is to tell people when you love them, because tomorrow is just a concept in our minds."

During that same show, Rosemary made a profound comment about listening. She said that we ask and ask and ask again for messages, for signs, for communication. Yet we rarely take the time to listen. How can we hear if we do not listen? And listening can take time. We need to be patient. And we need to be especially careful to listen for the messages of "coincidences."

It is a natural and normal human longing to want signs *now*, to want messages right away. However, listening is a skill and it takes time to develop such a skill.

As you practice being quiet, going within, taking the time to listen, and creating the space to listen, then you will hear. Then you will see the signs and receive the messages. At the same time, you will develop the art of patience.

❧ CHAPTER FOURTEEN ❧

Reaching Beyond Ourselves

Meditation and visualization will help you stop thinking so much and will help you begin a journey back. Healing will occur. You will begin to use your unused mind. You will see. You will understand. And you will grow wise. Then there will be peace.

Our hearts know the path to happiness and inner peace. Spiritual practices such as meditation and prayer remind us of what we already know. When we forget our heart's message and fall into life's ruts and crevices, we feel unfulfilled and unhappy. We get depressed and anxious. We have blurred our perspective, forgotten the bigger picture, and lost the way.

The remedy is simple. Take the time to remember your divinity, your spiritual nature. Remember why you are here. Meditation is one way of triggering your memory.

Meditation is the art or technique of quieting the mind so that the endless chatter that normally fills our consciousness is stilled. In the quiet of the silent mind, the meditator begins to become an observer, to reach a level of detachment, and, eventually, to become aware of a higher state of consciousness.

By pulling us out of the rut of our everyday awareness, meditation serves as a reminder of what we have been learning about higher, more spiritual values. To meditate regularly is to remember regularly. You are reminded of the bigger picture, of what is important to us in our lives and what is not.

It takes practice and discipline to rid the mind of its thousand everyday thoughts. I had to meditate daily for three months before I was able to reach a deeper awareness. It is important to be patient and to try not to get frustrated as you practice. Success at meditation does not happen overnight.

You do not need to sit in the lotus position in order to meditate. You can meditate while lying down, while sitting in a chair, or even while walking. The goal is to stop thinking, to observe and detach, to become mindful and aware.

As you teach yourself to meditate, you may find it helpful to try visualization and hypnosis as well. In both of these techniques, you are listening to a facilitator's voice, which may help you to focus your concentration.

Whether meditating, visualizing, or under hypnosis, you never give up control to someone else. No "forces" take over your mind or body. You do not enter a time machine. You are merely concentrating very deeply, and there is no danger whatsoever. In these states, you can be inspired, you can touch higher levels of awareness, you can be re-awakened to your divine nature. These are pathways to enlightenment.

Here is the essence of meditation. Every step you take is sacred; every breath you breathe is holy. If you understand and practice these precepts, you will be mindful and your consciousness will shift from the everyday to the "other" perspective. You will become observant, detached, and free from judgment.

*   *   *

I had been teaching a patient of mine, a business executive, how to meditate. At the beginning of one session, she remarked, "I just saw the most beautiful tree!"

"Where did you see the tree?" I asked.

"In front of my house," she replied. It had always been there.

When we learn to quiet our minds, we see the most beautiful things.

In my workshops I teach a simple meditation technique that requires only two minutes.

During the first minute, I instruct the group members to close their eyes and to take a few deep breaths and relax. For the next forty-five seconds, they are told to keep their minds completely quiet, to try not to think. Of course this is very difficult for most people. Our minds abhor emptiness, thus we fill them with ordinary thoughts, such as:

"My back hurts."

"I hear that person coughing."

"I never should have eaten that for breakfast."

These are not cosmic inspirations. We do not need these thoughts when we want our minds to be quiet, detached, observing.

During the second minute the group is instructed to imagine themselves sitting at the bottom of a beautiful pond. They can breathe perfectly normally.

"Every time you have a thought," I tell them, "put the thought in a bubble, watch the bubble float up to the surface of the pond and disappear. Then bring your mind back to quiet. If you have another thought, put it in another bubble and let that bubble float up and disappear. Keep repeating this process."

For people who are afraid of water, I tell them to imagine themselves sitting in a beautiful field and to use a buoyant helium balloon instead of a bubble.

For the next minute, they are using those bubbles and balloons.

They have begun to meditate.

This is called a bubble meditation, but you can use a word instead, focusing your mind on that word. If your mind wanders, gently and without judgment bring your attention back to the word.

The word you choose can be a neutral word, like the number one. Or it can be a Sanskrit word, which is called a mantra. Or it can be an emotionally loaded word, like the word *love*. Observe what feeling that evokes.

You can use a visual object instead, such as a candle or a flower. Or you can use an ancient technique of focusing on your breathing, counting each inhalation and exhalation.

Try the bubble meditation. You will be surprised by the benefits.

Group Exercises

I frequently do an exercise called "Faces" in my workshops. In a fairly dark room, with only enough light to prevent total darkness, I have people sitting in pairs. I lead them into a very relaxed, meditative state, and then they gaze gently into the face and features of their partner. This goes on for five to ten minutes. Features appear to change; people see age, race, and sex shifts. Sometimes animals or other metaphors are seen. People doing this exercise often receive psychic or intuitive information about the other person. Amazing things happen. The results are much more than perceptual distortion. Real information is received.

See what happens when you try this.

*   *   *

In Boston I led a large group of workshop participants in the Faces exercise. A woman from Boston and a woman from Milwaukee were partners. They had never met before that moment, seemingly randomly partnered from an audience of seven hundred.

They were sitting near the front, so I could see their faces as my eyes grew accustomed to the semi-darkness. A few tears were running from the eyes of the Boston woman.

After the exercise was over, and after the small groups of two or three had ample time to process the experience and to share their observations and feelings, I asked the woman if she would tell us what she had experienced during the exercise. She agreed.

"My tears were tears of joy," she explained. "I saw the face of my brother, and it has been a long time since I have seen him." Her older brother had been a soldier in World War II, and he had been killed in France when he was nineteen and a half years old.

Her partner then took the microphone. "Yesterday, during the large group regression, when you took all of us to our past lives, I had the experience of being a male soldier nineteen and a half years old, killed in France in World War Two."

She then provided details of that death, and she began to describe her partner's brother accurately.

Many people got goose bumps at that moment.

Afterwards I learned that the woman from Milwaukee was born on the same day that soldier was killed in France.

There really are no coincidences.

During a Faces exercise I was conducting in New York, an older man from India began weeping with happiness. He had just seen the face of a female Buddha in his partner, a young woman from New England whom he had never met until they had become partners ten minutes earlier.

"Female Buddhas are extremely rare!" he explained. Then his partner told us that for several years she had been a member of a small Buddhist sect that venerated a female Buddha.

These meaningful "coincidences" can help reorient us along our life's path, a path we have chosen even before we were born.

I am not sure why my workshops in Puerto Rico have always been so magical and filled with mystical experiences. Perhaps the enthusiasm, the open-mindedness, and the spirituality of the participants are responsible. In a packed auditorium at the Condado Plaza Hotel in San Juan in March 1998, miracles were happening once again.

Before the two-day workshop had begun and unbeknownst to me, a middle-aged woman who always wore a beautiful butterfly pendant on a thin golden chain around her neck had prayed to her son, who had died several months earlier.

"Give me a sign, a message," the grieving mother had asked. "I'll know it is you if you give me the sign of the butterfly."

Just before we began the Faces exercise, I had told the audience some touching stories about butterflies, as metaphors for the spirit, as symbols so frequently drawn by children who are dying or who know they are going to die (such as the numerous drawings of butterflies by children who died in the concentration camps of the Holocaust), and of actual butterflies hovering over people at funerals. I had not been planning to tell these stories. The thought of talking about butterflies had popped suddenly into my consciousness, and so I had begun to talk about butterflies.

The grieving mother smiled broadly. Her son had gotten the message to her. But the best was yet to come.

In the darkened room, we began the Faces exercise. I had instructed the group to choose as partners people they had never met before. The grieving mother's partner, another middle-aged woman who did not believe she possessed any psychic abilities, became aware of the spirit of a young man standing behind his mother. She described the young man to the mother, and told her specific details about his life, his personality, and his relationships.

His mother was shocked, excited, and ecstatic.

"Everything she said is perfectly accurate! She described him exactly!" The mother exclaimed.

Her face was now radiant, and I could actually see her breathing change and her shoulders lighten as the huge weight of her grief was gently lifted from her back.

As I taught the group this and other methods for opening avenues to their own psychic and intuitive abilities, many more amazing experiences were occurring all over the room. People in a small group on one side of the auditorium began tapping into and sharing the experiences of a distant group on the other side of the room. Incredible "coincidences" and synchronous events were occurring simultaneously among several groups in separate areas of the room. People with no previously recognized mastery of psychic processes were accurately describing the medical histories of complete strangers. People who had never met before that moment knew so much more about each other than could be possible in their usual state of consciousness.

As I watched these incredible interactions I silently marveled at how our minds are so much more powerful, sensitive, and aware than we think or know. We are amazing.

Psychics and mediums and gurus can be important to us, but only for a while. They can help us to see and to understand that there is so much more to our lives than we are usually aware. As I witnessed once again in Puerto Rico, we are all psychics, mediums, and gurus. As we learn, we open up and strengthen our own intuitive abilities, and we gain wisdom.

Psychometry

In this experiential exercise, which I usually conduct in groups of two, the participants exchange small objects belonging to them. The object may be a ring, a watch, a bracelet, keys, lockets, and so on. The item chosen should be one that is touched and handled primarily by its owner.

I begin the experience by doing a brief relaxation exercise, which helps the participants to focus and to quiet their minds. With their eyes closed as they remain in a relaxed state, the two people hold their partner's object gently in their hands. The participants are instructed to become aware of any thoughts, feelings, impressions, or sensations that come into their awareness.

The impressions may be psychological (feelings, moods, or emotions), physical (bodily sensations), psychic (visions, messages, thoughts, childhood or past-life scenes), or spiritual (messages or images from other dimensions).

After about five minutes have elapsed, I instruct the group to share every aspect of the experience with their partner. It is very important to share every sensation, thought, and impression, even if it seems silly or weird, because these are often the most accurate and powerful "hits." Frequently the validation of one of these strange impressions is immediate and most meaningful.

Whether it is the energy of the object being held that facilitates the intuitive transfer of information or the relaxed focusing of the mind, the net result is an awakening and a validation of the intuitive ability we all possess.

This exercise is safe, simple, instructive, and a lot of fun.

Energy Scanning

Whatever impression or sensation emerges into your awareness is valid. In this exercise, let your imagination run free.
This is all for learning and growth.

Before working in groups of two, the participants practice
becoming aware of their own energy fields. With their eyes
gently closed and in a relaxed state, they are instructed to
bring their hands together slowly, palms facing each other, beginning with the hands about two feet apart. As their hands
draw together, people often become aware of tingling in their
palms, of increasing heat or thermal changes, and of a subtle
resistance, like some sort of malleable barrier felt before the
hands actually touch. This beginning exercise is repeated several times.

In groups of two, the "receiver" slowly scans the body of his
or her partner, who stands or sits quietly during the exercise.
The scanning is done by the hands, at a distance of several
inches or more from the body of the other person. The scanner does not actually touch the partner.

The entire body should be scanned from all sides, and the
scanner should become aware of any temperature changes,
such as areas of heat or cold. Any thoughts, sensations, or impressions are noted and remembered. Any variations in the energy field should also be acknowledged.

After several minutes, the roles are reversed. The scanner
becomes the quiet "subject" and the former subject becomes
the scanner or receiver. After repeating the process, the partners then spend several minutes sharing the entire experience,
with all of their observations.

Often stunningly accurate medical diagnoses are made during this exercise. Confidential information can be somehow
transferred to the scanner. Our intuitive minds once again can
be activated during this brief experiential exercise.

Brief Visualization Exercises

Hypnosis is merely focused concentration. There is nothing mysterious or sinister about it. Close your eyes and imagine that you are biting into a big, juicy lemon. Use all of your senses. Taste the lemon. Smell it. See it. Bite more deeply.

People often make a "lemon face" with puckered lips when I ask them to do this. They are tasting the lemon. I didn't stick a lemon in their mouths. They were tapping their memory banks.

If you tasted the lemon, you were just hypnotized.

Extend your arms straight out in front of you with your palms up. Do not bend your arms at the elbows.

After you close your eyes, imagine that I am placing a big, heavy book into your left hand. And now a second heavy book into your left hand. And then imagine I am tying a big, buoyant helium balloon to your right hand. A third heavy book now goes into your left hand, and then a second helium balloon is tied to your right hand. Keep your arms exactly where they are now and open your eyes.

The body as well as the mind is involved in the hypnotic process.

Over the past two hundred years or so with the emergence and spread of the Age of Enlightenment, people have overemphasized the role of logic and science in human relationships, culture, health, and philosophy. We have developed the notion that science will be able to cure all of our ills and problems.

In fact, we have become unbalanced because of this thinking. We have neglected intuitive wisdom, the heart, the creative and inspired impulse. We have glorified technology, but our ethics, our morality, and our spiritual growth have not advanced at the same pace. We now find ourselves in the position where our technology has advanced enough to destroy the planet, and people who are not wise or enlightened have their fingers on the button.

Technology and science are neutral. It is what people do with them, how they are applied and the circumstances under which they are used, that determines their value. We have learned that science cannot cure all the ills of humankind. Only wise, loving, compassionate, and responsible leaders can accomplish that goal.

So the pendulum must swing back. Not all the way back to superstition and fear, but back to the midpoint, the place of harmony and balance. Back to the position where science and intuition are perfectly blended, where heart and mind are one, working harmoniously to bring us peace and health.

It is important to know how intuition works.

Even before I had witnessed him give healing messages to the woman with the rose garden and her husband's ring, I had the opportunity to observe James Van Praagh at a workshop in New Orleans. He provided accurate details about deceased loved ones to their surviving families and friends. Four hundred people crowded the room. James would get an image or a message, convey that message to the large group, and with another detail or two, someone would stand, confirming the accuracy of the message.

I was sitting in the back, quietly trying to do what James was doing. I was trying to anticipate his questions, comments, and messages, but my accuracy was minimal. Was he somehow leading them? Was he being general enough so that somebody in such a large group was bound to fit his comments? Was he exceptionally adept at reading body language?

He was getting this information, this knowledge, from somewhere other than the audience, and he was helping people heal their grief. Oh well, I thought, there are a few talented people in the world who could somehow tap into this stuff. I certainly wasn't one of them.

Two weeks later I was conducting an experiential workshop on spirituality and past-life regression therapy to an audience of seven hundred in West Palm Beach, Florida. In response to a question from someone in the audience, I tried to explain how a medium works by formulating an example.

"It works like this," I said, beginning to imagine a scene. "The medium might say: 'I'm aware of a young man named Robert. He's nineteen or twenty years old, and he died in a car accident. He wants you to know that he's fine, he's well, that he loves you very much and that you shouldn't grieve so much for him. He's well and he is still around you. Also, he wanted you to give the black leather jacket that was hanging in his closet to Gary.'" I had made up this whole scene.

Then I moved on to talk about other topics.

Unbeknownst to me, Carole, sitting in the back of the room thought, I hope he heard James Van Praagh tell that story, because it has something to do with someone in the audience.

After the workshop ended, I was signing some books when two women, one misty-eyed, came up to me.

"Where did you get that story about Robert and the car accident?" the tearful one softly inquired.

I told her that I made up the whole thing.

"No you didn't," she answered firmly. "My brother, Robert, was killed in a car accident when he was twenty years old. We have missed him so much. I just gave his black leather jacket, which had been hanging in his closet, to our younger brother, Gary. I felt he wanted me to do this."

We are spiritual beings within these human forms. The spiritual part of us never dies. We never really lose our loved ones. Thus, we can all do what I did, because we are all connected.

In meditative states and in dreams I continue to experience vivid metaphorical images and to intuit thought-provoking insights. I frequently receive answers to questions or dilemmas that, like pearls forming in oysters, are irritating the depths of my subconscious mind.

In one such powerful but seemingly simplistic image, I saw how people view themselves as separate entities, and yet in reality, we all are eternally connected to each other. I glimpsed a vast sea filled with ice cubes. Each ice cube was distinct, with fixed and definite boundaries, yet all floated in the same freezing water. Soon the water warmed, and the ice cubes melted. *Everything* was the water. Every ice cube was connected to every other ice cube in the sea. Then the heat increased, and the water began to boil, transforming into steam. Soon all was steam, silent and invisible. Yet the steam contained what was once the water and the ice cubes. The only difference between the states of ice, water, and steam was the vibrational energy of the molecules.

Humankind thinks of itself as physically separate, like the ice cubes. In reality, however, we all are the same interconnected substance.

You can have past-life experiences through means other than hypnosis. My first two past-life journeys occurred through bodywork and in a dream.

My first experience happened spontaneously during a shiatsu, or acupressure, treatment. In this vivid visual tableau, I saw myself as an ancient priest, taller and thinner than I am now. I was standing in an oddly shaped geometric building, flat on the top with sloping sides. I kept hearing the word *ziggurat* in my mind, but at that time I did not know what this meant.

The priest had a great deal of power, but instead of using his position to teach spiritual truths, he was instead focused on obtaining even more power and wealth. As I wistfully looked into his future, I could see that his values never shifted to the spiritual, even though priests were free to teach spiritual truths as long as the needs of the royalty were also met.

I gradually returned to full waking consciousness. At home later that day I looked up the word *ziggurat*. There it was in the encyclopedia. In the Babylonian period of history, a millennium before Christ, temples of that same geometric shape I had seen in my vision were called ziggurats.

A few years later I had a second past-life experience, this time in a dream. It occurred on the second night of a five-day training for professionals that I was teaching. All the participants were staying in the same hotel, and the intensity of the sessions was exhausting.

In the dream, which was one of those vivid dreams where you remember every detail, I was again a priest, this time a Catholic priest somewhere in Europe several centuries ago. I was in a dungeon. One of my arms was chained to the wall in back of me. I was being tortured and then killed for teaching heretical, forbidden things.

I awakened, but in a hypnagogic state, and the dream continued for a while. I could still see and feel the images as I lay on the bed in a completely darkened room. Then I became aware of an inner voice or message.

"When you had the chance to teach the truth, you did not."

I knew the reference was to the Babylonian priest, who did not teach spiritual truths.

"When you did not have the chance, you did. . . . You . . . forced the issue."

I knew the Catholic priest could have safely taught about love and compassion. He did not need to get himself killed by challenging the harsh authorities of that time.

"This time get it right," the voice gently concluded.

I could not fall back to sleep. Finally I went down to breakfast. One of the students taking my course was a well-known professor of psychiatry at a distinguished university.

"You look terrible," she observed as she stood next to me.

"I know," I answered. "I didn't sleep well last night."

"I know that," she responded. "I looked into your dream!"

I didn't believe this was possible, and, sensing my skepticism, she elaborated.

"My family has had mediumistic abilities on my mother's side for many generations," she explained. "I also have these abilities."

I was intrigued now, so I asked her what she had seen.

"I saw you as a Catholic priest in Scotland centuries ago. You were imprisoned. Your right arm was chained to the wall behind you, and you were tortured and killed for teaching about reincarnation." She was more specific than I had been.

There was more.

"You have to be careful. Some of those people are back again now!" she added.

So I keep my eyes open.

CHAPTER FIFTEEN

God and Religion

They tell me there are many gods, for God is in each of us.

There is only one religion and that is love.

We must remember, too, that the transcendent Being is the only cause, the father and the creator of the universe. That He fills all things not with His thought only but with His essence.

His essence is not exhausted in the universe. He is above it and beyond.

We may say that only His powers are in the universe. But while He is above His powers, He includes them. What they do, He does through them.

From time to time, in letters, at conferences, or on radio call-in shows, people have asked me where God is in my writings. This question always surprises me, because to me God is everywhere in my writings, not only identified by the name God, but in so many other ways as well. Every time you find the word *love,* I am talking about God. We all have God within us.

It may seem strange to hear a psychiatrist talking about God and love. Yet I must, because the foundations of spiritual psychotherapy require the recognition of our divinity, the real nature of our souls, and the true purpose of existence here in physical form. Only in this way can we see the bigger picture.

Without love and without God, there is nothing.

God does not require our respect. We persist in personifying God despite our knowledge that God is far beyond what we can even begin to conceptualize.

God has no sex. Another personification.

God has no religion. We all know this in our hearts.

God has no race.

God is everything, a loving energy possessing incomprehensible wisdom, power, and unknowable qualities. We are all composed of God, for God is in each of us, the substance of our being.

God is even beyond the steam that contains the potential of the water, that contains the potential of the ice.

God is unseen, unknowable yet containing the potential of everything.

There is a joke going around about a devout and pious man whose life was being endangered by a flood. The waters were rising rapidly, and he was forced to take refuge on the roof of his house. Still, the waters kept rising.

Finally a police boat came to rescue him from his roof. "Get in the boat," the policeman shouted.

"No," he responded. "I have lived my whole life as a devout and charitable man. God will protect me."

"Don't be foolish," answered the policeman. "Get in the boat. The waters are still rising, and you are in great danger!"

The man continued to refuse, and the boat left.

The waters did indeed continue to rise. Twice more the rescue boat returned, and twice more the man refused to board it.

"God will protect me," he insisted, filled with confidence. The boat left to rescue others.

Soon the flood waters engulfed the entire house and its roof. The man drowned.

In heaven he encountered God. Furious that God had not rescued him, the man complained loudly.

"All my life I have been devout. I have obeyed all the commandments. I have given large sums to charity. And the only time I asked for anything, you abandoned me!"

"But I sent the boat three times," God explained. "Why didn't you get in?"

For far too many years, for untold centuries and millennia, God and religion have been misunderstood, distorted, and consciously manipulated by mankind. God's name, perhaps the ultimate symbol of peace, love, and compassion, has been invoked to wage countless wars, murders, and genocide. Even today, as the twenty-first century begins to unfold, "holy" wars infect our planet like a medieval plague. How can a war ever be holy? This is a contradiction of terms, a horrid oxymoron, an absolute sin, superficially disguised by a manipulative rationalization.

God is peace; God is love. We have forgotten that, since we are created in the divine image, God is within our hearts, and that we are also creatures of peace, beings of love and divinity. There can be only one religion, because there is only one God, the God of us all. We must love one another, because love is the way home. Otherwise, like stubborn schoolchildren, we will be doomed to repeat grade after grade, until we learn the lesson of love.

Only by letting go of our fears, by seeing those people of

other religions as our equals, as fellow souls on the road to heaven, can we be truly loving, in an unconditional sense. We are all the same; we are all rowing the same boat. In our many incarnations, we ourselves have been all religions, all races. The soul has no race, no religion. It knows only love and compassion.

When we know that we are all the same, that there are only superficial and unimportant differences among us but no difference that *really* matters, then we can reach back and help everyone along the path, no matter whether they are like us or not.

When you dig beneath the surface rituals and customs of the various religions, you find an amazing similarity of ideas, concepts, and advice. Even the words are incredibly similar.[*] We have been killing each other in the name of religion when, at the deeper levels, many of the most devout actually believe the same thing.

All of the great religions place a common emphasis on the importance of leading a spiritual life, of understanding the divine presence in and beyond all beings and things, of good deeds and service, of love and compassion and charity and hope and faith. All describe a life after death and the immortality of the soul. All stress kindness, forgiveness, and peace.

When I talk about religions, I am referring to the wonderful spiritual wisdom and traditions, not to the man-made edicts and rules that were promulgated for political reasons and which serve to separate people rather than to unify them. We must be careful to differentiate spiritual truths from politically motivated rules. Such rules are fences, keeping us fearful and apart.

Now, we can begin to accept concepts of divine omnipres-

---

[*]See Appendix A for examples of shared spiritual values in the world's great religions.

ence, of the immortality of the soul, of continued existence after physical death, on the basis of data, not only on faith.

So why are we so ignorant of the essence of our own religions, with their rich spiritual traditions, let alone the religions of our friends and neighbors? Why do we insist on seeing only the differences, when the similarities are overwhelming? Why do we ignore the teachings, the precepts, the rules, and the guidelines that were so lovingly and brilliantly presented by the great teachers?

Again, I think we have forgotten what we know. Caught in the rut of everyday life, we are so consumed with worry and anxiety, so concerned with our status, our exteriors, with what others think of us, that we have forgotten our spiritual selves. We are fearful of death because we have forgotten about our true nature. We are so worried about our reputations and positions, about being manipulated by others for their "gain" and our "loss," we are so terrified of appearing stupid, that we have lost the courage to be spiritual.

Yet science and spirituality, long considered antithetical, are coming together. Physicists and psychiatrists are becoming the mystics of the modern time. We are confirming what prior mystics knew intuitively. We are all divine beings. We have known this for thousands of years, but we have forgotten. And to return home, we have to remember the way.

If there is only one God and only one religion, which is love, why should we practice the religion of our birth, or choose any single faith over another?

In the end, it doesn't matter what sort of church or temple we attend, if indeed we choose to attend at all. Like spokes on a bicycle wheel, all paths dictated by the great religions lead to the same center, to godliness and enlightenment. One path is no better or worse than the other. They are all equal.

However, being steeped in the wisdom and truths of your religion since your early childhood provides not only a significant head start—you have already accumulated a great deal of knowledge and experience—but it also provides a comfortable familiarity. Familiarity brings a sense of peace. Your mind relaxes and, almost without conscious effort, you can enter a deeper meditative state. Familiarity and comfort lessen distractions and allow your mind to focus, to slip much more smoothly into deeper levels of meditation, prayer, and contemplation. In this deep state, you can experience transcendent levels of consciousness.

There are great truths and beauty and wisdom in all the great religious traditions. You should sample them all, like a student, because an important insight that a shift in spiritual perspective can bring can accelerate your spiritual progress. There is no need to abandon your tradition. After all, some people prefer roses, others orchids or lilies or wildflowers or sunflowers. But they are all beautiful in their own right, and God causes the same sun to shine on them all; the same rain nourishes them. They are different, but all are special.

To paraphrase a teaching found in all spiritual disciplines, the rain falls on the weeds as well as on the flowers, and the sun shines on prisons as well as on churches.

God's light does not discriminate, and neither should ours.

There is not one path, one way, one church, one ideology.

There is only one light.

When the fences come down, all the flowers can bloom together in a garden of unparalleled magnificence, an Eden on the earth.

❧ CHAPTER SIXTEEN ❧

Finding Your Way Home

Patience and timing . . . everything comes when it must come. A life cannot be rushed, cannot be worked on a schedule as so many people want it to be. We must accept what comes to us at a given time, and not ask for more. But life is endless, so we never die; we were never really born. We just pass through different phases. There is no end. Humans have many dimensions. But time is not as we see time, but rather in lessons that are learned.

As I wrote in the beginning of this book, people are always asking me if I've had more contact with the Masters. By now you can see that the messages from the Masters come from everywhere. Some of the messages come from my own meditations and some of the information comes through feelings, at a level of understanding that is very difficult to translate into words. For some concepts, there are no words.

Much of the knowledge comes through examples and experiences, as I have described in all four books. There is a complete and coherent spiritual philosophy in the quotes, the words, the stories, and the reflections. The answers are there, but we often do not take the time to see, to digest, to understand.

Only love is real. Love is an energy of incredible power and strength. We are all made of this energy.

Love is an absolute. Love never ends, never stops. The purest form is unconditional love, expressing your love and expecting nothing in return. By giving love away freely you become a spiritual millionaire.

Remember to listen to your intuitions, and try not to let your fears sway the soft and gentle murmurings of your beautiful heart. Feel the freedom to love without holding back, without reserve, without condition. For our lives on this plane are limited ones. We are merely in a school. When we return home, we take only our thoughts, our actions, our love, with us.

Finally, do not be afraid. We are immortal, eternal spirits and we are always loved. In fact, we *are* love.

APPENDIX A

Shared Spiritual Values

Here are some passages from the sacred writings of some of the world's great religions. These quotes demonstrate that there is really only one religion, when you transcend the surface rituals and reach the spiritual treasures lying beyond. In this section on the unity of all the great religions, I have been benefited by the wonderful book *Oneness: Great Principles Shared by All Religions*, by Jeffrey Moses.

Responsibility for One's Actions

Buddhism

It is nature's rule, that as we sow, we shall reap.

Christianity

Whatever a man sows, that he will also reap. . . . God will render to every man according to his deeds.

Hinduism

Thou canst not gather what thou dost not sow; as thou dost plant the tree so it will grow.

Judaism

A liberal man will be enriched, and one who waters will himself be watered.

Forgiveness

Buddhism

Never is hate diminished by hatred. It is only diminished by love—This is an eternal law.

Christianity

For if you forgive others the wrongs they have done, your heavenly Father will also forgive you; but if you do not forgive others, then the wrongs you have done will not be forgiven by your Father. . . . "Lord, how often shall my brother sin against me, and I forgive him? As many as seven times?" Jesus said to him, "I do not say to you seven times, but seventy times seven."

Hinduism

The noble-minded dedicate themselves to the promotion of peace and the happiness of others—even those who injure them.

Islam

Forgive thy servant seventy times a day.

Judaism

The most beautiful thing a man can do is to forgive wrong.

Peace and Love

Buddhism

You reap the things you sowed. . . . This is the Law. . . . The heart of it is Love; the end of it is Peace.

Conquer your foe by force, and you increase his anger. Conquer by love, and you will reap no after-sorrow. . . . Him I call indeed a Brah-

mana who utters true speech, instructive and free from harshness, so that he offends no one.

When righteousness is practiced to win peace, he who so walks shall gain the victory and all fetters utterly destroy.

Hurt none by word or deed, be consistent in well-doing.

Christianity

Do not set yourself against the man who wrongs you. If someone slaps you on the right cheek, turn and offer him your left. If a man wants to sue you for your shirt, let him have your coat as well. Blessed are the peacemakers: for they shall be called the children of God. . . . The peace of God, which passeth all understanding, shall keep your hearts and minds.

Love your enemies, bless those who curse you, do good to those who hate you, and pray for your persecutors; only so can you be children of your heavenly Father, who makes his sun rise on good and bad alike, and sends the rain on the honest and the dishonest. If you love only those who love you, what reward can you expect?

"Love the Lord your God with all your heart, with all your soul, with all your mind." That is the greatest commandment. It comes first. The second is like it: "Love your neighbor as yourself." Everything in the Law and the prophets hangs on these two commandments.

This is my commandment to you: Love one another.

Hinduism

The mind is restless and hard to restrain, but it may be restrained by practice and absence of desire. To whatsoever object the inconstant mind goes out [one] should subdue it, bring it back, and place it upon the

Spirit. Supreme bliss surely cometh to the sage whose mind is thus at peace.

With kindness conquer rage, with goodness malice; with generosity defeat all meanness; with the straight truth defeat lies and deceit.

Islam

Recompense evil, conquer it, with good. . . . Shall I tell you what acts are better than fasting, charity, and prayers? Making peace between enemies are such acts; for enmity and malice tear up the heavenly rewards by the roots.

Judaism

How beautiful upon the mountains are the feet of him who brings good tidings, who publishes peace.

But I say unto you: Deeds of love are worth as much as all the commandments of the law. . . . Not learning but doing is the chief thing.

Love is the beginning and end of the Torah.

Thou shalt love thy neighbor as thyself.

The Golden Rule

Buddhism

Hurt not others with that which pains yourself.

Full of love for all things in the world, practicing virtue in order to benefit others, this man alone is happy.

Judge not thy neighbor.

Christianity

Pass no judgment, and you will not be judged. . . . Always treat others as you would like them to treat you: that is the Law and the prophets. . . . The gate that leads to life is small and the road is narrow.

Hinduism

This is the sum of all true righteousness—Treat others, as thou wouldst thyself be treated.

Do nothing to thy neighbor, which hereafter Thou wouldst not have thy neighbor do to thee.

A man obtains a proper rule of action by looking on his neighbor as himself.

Islam

Do unto all men as you would wish to have done unto you; and reject for others what you would reject for yourselves.

Judaism

What is hurtful to yourself do not to your fellow man. That is the whole of the Torah and the remainder is but commentary.

Judge not thy neighbor till thou art in his place.

Spiritual Values

Buddhism

Like a beautiful flower, full of color, but without scent, are the fine but fruitless words of him who does not act accordingly.

The real treasure is that laid up by a man or woman through charity and piety, temperance, and self-control. . . . The treasure thus hid is secure and does not pass away.

Christianity

You must therefore be all goodness, just as your heavenly Father is all good. . . . Do not store up for yourselves treasure on earth . . . store up treasure in heaven: you cannot serve God and money. For what is a man profited if he shall gain the whole world and lose his own soul? . . . Man shall not live by bread alone, but by every word of God.

Is there a man of you who by anxious thought can add a foot to his height or a day to his life? Set your mind on God's kingdom and his justice before everything else, and all the rest will come to you as well.

If you wish to enter life, keep the commandments. . . . Do not murder; do not commit adultery; do not steal; do not give false evidence; honor your father and mother; and love your neighbor as yourself. . . . If you wish to go the whole way, sell your possessions, and give to the poor, and then you will have riches in heaven. . . . It is easier for a camel to pass through the eye of a needle than for a rich man to enter the kingdom of God. . . . But many who are first will be last, and the last first.

Hinduism

Seek this wisdom by doing service, by strong search, by questions, and by humility. . . . There is no purifier in this world, to be compared to spiritual knowledge. Say what is true! Do thy duty. Do not swerve from the truth.

He who acts righteously is wise. . . . Man lives not by material bread alone. . . . Do not hurt others, do no one injury by thought or deed, utter no word to pain thy fellow creatures. . . . He who gives up anger attains to God.

Islam

Dost thou know who is the rejector of faith? The one who neglects the orphan. And never advocates the feeding of the poor. . . . Therefore, woe to those who observe the "salat" prayers while heedless of their "salat." They only show off. And are averse to charity. . . . Ye shall be charitable, for Allah loves the charitable.

Ye shall not take each other's money dishonestly. . . . Do not confound the truth with falsehoods nor shall you conceal the truth knowingly. . . . Allah is omnipresent, omniscient.

The human being is in total loss. Except those who believe and lead a righteous life, and exhort each other to uphold the truth and exhort each other to be steadfast.

A man asked Mohammed how to tell when one is truly faithful, and he replied: "If you derive pleasure from the good which you do and are grieved by the evil which you commit, then you are a true believer."

Seek knowledge from the cradle to the grave.

Judaism

Thou shalt not murder. Neither shalt thou commit adultery. Neither shalt thou steal. Neither shalt thou bear false witness. . . . Neither shalt thou covet.

Who shall ascend the mountain of the Lord? And who shall stand in His holy place? He that has clean hands and a pure heart; who has not set his mind on what is false, and has not sworn deceitfully.

Speak ye every man truth to his neighbor; execute the judgment of truth and peace in your gates. . . . Blessed is he that considereth the poor: the Lord will deliver him in time of trouble.

Man doth not live by bread only, but by every word that proceedeth out of the mouth of the Lord.

Immortality

Buddhism

The Self is the Lord of Self. . . . When a man subdues well his self, he will find a Lord very difficult to find . . . knowing that this body is like froth, knowing that its nature is that of a mirage, the disciple passes untouched by death. . . . He in whom the desire for the Ineffable has arisen, whose mind is permeated by that desire, whose thoughts are not distracted by lower desires, he is named "Bound upstream."

Christianity

That the dead are raised to life again is shown by Moses himself in the story of the burning bush, when he calls the Lord, "the God of Abraham, Isaac, and Jacob." God is not God of the dead but of the living; for him we all are alive.

You are gods. Those are called gods to whom the word of God was delivered. . . . No one who is alive and has faith shall ever die.

Hinduism

That knowledge which through the soul is a realization of both the known and the knower is . . . wisdom. . . . Whenever anything is produced, it is due to the union of the body and the soul. The deluded do not see the spirit when it quitteth or remains in the body.

Deep within abides another life, not like the life of the senses, escaping sight, unchanging. This endures when all created things have passed away.

The individual soul is nothing else in essence than universal soul. . . . Human beings all are as head, arms, trunk, and legs unto one another.

Islam

Riches are not from an abundance of worldly goods, but from a contented mind. Whatever good you do for others, you send it before your own soul and shall find it with God, who seest all you do.

Judaism

The Lord is my shepherd; I shall not want. He maketh me to lie down in green pastures . . . he restoreth my soul. . . . Yea though I walk through the valley of the shadow of death, I will fear no evil, for Thou art with me. . . . Surely goodness and mercy shall follow me all the days of my life; and I shall dwell in the house of the Lord forever.

The Universal God

Buddhism

If you think the Law is outside yourself, you are embracing not the absolute Law but some inferior teaching.

He that loveth not, knoweth not God. For God is love.

Christianity

God is love, and he who abides in love abides in God, and God abides in him. . . . Know ye not that ye are the temple of God, and that the spirit of God dwelleth in you?

For in fact the kingdom of God is within you. There is one God and Father of all, who is above all, and through all, and in you all.

Hinduism

As a single sun illuminateth the whole world, even so, does the One Spirit illumine every body. In those for whom knowledge of the true Self has dispersed ignorance, the Supreme, as if lighted by the sun, is revealed.

He is the one God hidden in all beings, all-pervading, the Self within all beings, watching over all worlds, dwelling in all beings, the witness, the perceiver. . . . God hides hidden in the hearts of all.

Islam

On God's own nature has been molded man's. . . . All creatures are the family of God; and he is the most beloved of God who does most good unto His family.

Judaism

Hear, O Israel: The Lord our God, the Lord is One. And thou shalt love the Lord thy God with all thy heart, and with all thy soul, and with all thy might.

Love the Lord your God. . . . Serve Him with all your heart, and with all your soul, that I will give the rain of your land in its season . . . and I will give grass in thy fields for thy cattle, and thou shalt eat and be satisfied. And ye shall teach them [these words] to your children, talking of them when thou sittest in thy house, and when thou walkest by the way, and when thou liest down, and when thou risest up . . . that your days be multiplied.

Have we not all one Father? Has not one God created us? . . . God created man in His own image, in the image of God created He him.

APPENDIX B

Longer Meditation Exercises

The two meditations in this section will help you to feel more peace in your life by removing the blocks and obstacles to your inner joy and happiness.

You can work with a partner, one reading the script to the other, who is relaxing with closed eyes. Or you can record the script into a tape recorder, later playing it back to yourself as you become the listener. *But never play this tape in your car.*

Before you start the exercise, lie down on a bed or sit in a comfortable chair and loosen any tight-fitting clothes. Make sure there will be no distractions or interruptions. Kick off your shoes; take off your glasses; take out your contact lenses. Allow yourself to relax completely. Do not cross your legs. You might want to play soft, gentle music in the background if music is soothing to you.

Whatever images, feelings, sensations, or thoughts come into your awareness are fine. Try not to censor, judge, or analyze. You can do that later. While listening, just let yourself experience whatever comes up.

Do not be concerned about what is memory, fantasy, imagination, metaphor, or symbol. Or any combination of all of these. It does not matter. You will feel better anyway.

Read the script in a calm and slow voice, pausing slightly when you come to three ellipses (. . .) and pausing for a longer time when the direction to pause is in brackets. (Note: Read the directions in brackets to yourself, not out loud.) Before you read the script to someone else or before you record it, you may want to practice reading the script several times to find a rhythm that is comfortable for you and that allows enough time for you to respond to the instructions.

Do not hurry the process. There is no time limit on this exercise; you cannot take too long to do it.

Practice these exercises. The more you meditate, the deeper you will go and the more experiences you will have.

Most people handle and integrate the material without difficulty. They actually feel much better. The risks of a disturbing reaction, such as anxiety or guilt, are minimal. If this happens, however, you might want to see a therapist and resolve any problems that might have occurred.

Meditation 1:
Through the Door into Past Lives

With your eyes gently closed, take a few deep breaths. Imagine that you can breathe out the tensions and stresses in your body. . . . Imagine that you can breathe in the beautiful energy all around you. . . .

Let each breath take you deeper and deeper into a beautiful state of relaxation.

[Pause for fifteen seconds to allow the breath to relax the body.]

Now relax all your muscles. Relax the muscles of your face and jaw. Let go of all tightness and all tension in these muscles. . . .

Relax the muscles of your neck and your shoulders. . . .

Relax your arms. . . . Completely relax the muscles of your back, both the upper back and the lower back. . . . Let go of all tightness and all tension in these muscles.

Relax the muscles of your stomach and abdomen, so that your breathing stays perfectly relaxed. . . .

Relax completely the muscles of your legs, so that now your entire body is in a state of deep peace. . . .

Let any outside noises or distractions only deepen your level even more.

Imagine or visualize or feel a beautiful light above your head. You can choose the color or colors. This light will deepen your level and heal your body. . . .

Let the light flow into your body through the top of your head. It illuminates the brain and spinal cord, healing these tissues and deepening your level even more. . . .

Let the light flow down, from above to below, like a beautiful wave of light, touching every cell, every fiber, and every organ in your body with peace and love and healing. . . .

Wherever your body needs healing, let the light be very strong and powerful in this area. . . . [Fifteen-second pause.]

And let the rest of the light flow all the way to your feet, so that your body is filled with this beautiful light. . . .

Now, imagine or feel the light completely surrounding the outside of your body as well, as if you were wrapped in a beautiful bubble or cocoon of light. This protects you, heals your skin, and deepens your level even more. . . .

Counting backwards from ten to one, let each number back take you deeper into the relaxed state.

Ten . . . Nine . . . Eight . . . Deeper and deeper with each number back . . .

Seven . . . Six . . . Five . . . More and more peaceful and relaxed . . .

Four . . . Three . . . So calm and serene . . .

Two . . . Nearly there . . .

One . . . Good.

In this wonderful state of peace and tranquillity, imagine yourself walking down a beautiful staircase . . . down, down . . . deeper and deeper . . . down, down . . . each step down deepening your level even more. . . .

As you reach the bottom of the steps, in front of you is a beautiful garden . . . a garden of peace and beauty and safety . . . a sanctuary. . . .

Walk into this garden and find a place to rest. . . .

Your body, still filled by the light and surrounded by the light, continues to heal and to recuperate. The deepest levels of your mind can open up. You can remember everything. You can experience all levels of your multidimensional self. You are far greater than your body or your brain.

If you are ever uncomfortable with any memory or any feeling or any experience during this meditation, just float above it and watch from a distance, as if you were watching a movie. If you are still uncomfortable, float back to the garden and rest there, or even open your eyes and return to full, waking consciousness.

If you are not uncomfortable, stay with the images and the feelings. You are always in control.

In this state of deep relaxation your memory is enhanced. You can remember everything, every experience you have ever had, in this body or any other body you have had. . . .

To show you this, let us go back in time, at first a little bit, and then more and more.

As I count backwards from five to one, remember a recent pleasant meal. Use all of your senses, sight and sound, touch and taste and smell. Experience vividly and pay attention to details.

Five . . . Four . . . You can remember everything. . . .

Three . . . Remembering a recent pleasant meal. . . .

Two . . . Let it come into complete focus. . . .

One . . . Be there, and for a few moments re-experience this meal. . . .

Is anybody with you? . . . Let yourself remember. [Fifteen-second pause.]

You can remember far more than a meal. Counting backwards again from five to one, remember a memory from your childhood. Keep this memory a pleasant one, if you wish . . . a pleasant childhood memory.

Always remember that if you are ever uncomfortable with any memory, just float above it and watch from a distance, as if watching a movie. Or even float back to the garden, if you wish, and rest. If you are very uncomfortable, just open your eyes, and you will be completely awake and alert.

Five . . . Going all the way back to a pleasant childhood memory.

Four . . . You can remember everything.

Three . . . Two . . . Let it come into complete focus.

One . . . Be there and experience this again. . . . [One-minute pause.]

And you can remember even more than a childhood memory. Counting backwards again from five to one, remember before you were born . . . in utero . . . in your mother's womb.

Pay attention to any sensations or impressions, physical, emotional, or spiritual. You may experience events outside the body. Or you may become aware of your mother's feelings and thoughts, since you are so closely bonded at this time. Whatever comes into your awareness is fine.

Five . . . Going all the way back to the in-utero time, in your mother's womb. . . .

Four . . . You can remember everything. . . .

Three . . . Two . . . Coming into complete focus . . .

One . . . Be there, and re-experience this environment. . . . [One-minute pause.]

If you wish, you can observe the birth, but with no pain or discomfort. . . . See who is around and how you are received . . . with no pain, just observing. . . . [Fifteen-second pause.]

Now float above and leave that time. . . .

Imagine a beautiful door in front of you. . . . This is a door through time and space, a door into your past lives or spiritual state. There is something for you to learn on the other side of this door . . . something that will help you in your present life.

Counting backwards from five to one, the door will open. It will pull you; it will attract you. Go to the door. You will see a beautiful light on the other side of the door. Go through the door and into the light. Go through the light and join the scene, the person, the experience on the other side of the light. Let it come into complete focus on the count of one.

The door opens. . . . It pulls you. . . . Go to it. . . . Go through the door and into the light.

Five . . . Going all the way back to your past lives . . .

Four . . . You can remember everything. . . . Go through the light. . . .

Three . . . You become aware of the scene, a person, an experience on the other side of the light. . . .

Two . . . Coming into complete focus . . .

One . . . Be there!

If you find yourself in a body, look down at your feet. . . . What kind of footwear, if any, do you have? Pay attention to details. . . .

What are your clothes like? . . .

Are your skin and hands different? . . .

Go to the significant scenes and events of this life. . . . You can move forward or backwards in time. . . . See what happens to you . . . what becomes of you. . . . [Thirty-second pause.]

If you find other people, look into their faces, into their eyes. . . . Do you recognize them? . . .

You may feel or hear or know rather than see. Your memories do not have to be visual. . . .

Go to the other significant events of this experience. . . . [One-minute pause.]

Now move to the end of that time, of that experience, and observe what happens to you. . . . [Fifteen-second pause.]

Who is around? . . . [Fifteen-second pause.]

Now float above and leave that scene. . . .

Review. . . . What did you learn? . . . What were the lessons of that experience? . . . [Fifteen-second pause.]

How do these lessons connect to the present time? . . . [Fifteen-second pause.]

Imagine that a beautiful and loving being, like an angel, can come and be with you for a while. You can communicate, whether through words . . . thoughts . . . feelings . . . visions . . . or in any other way. . . .

Are there any messages for you? . . .

Is there any knowledge you need to take back with you? . . . [Thirty-second pause.]

If you wish, ask a question and listen for the answer. . . . [Thirty-second pause.]

Your body in the garden has been filled with the beautiful light. It has been healing and refreshing.

Now it is time to return to full waking consciousness.

Counting upwards from one to ten. Let each number up awaken you more and more. By the count of ten you can open your eyes and you will be wide awake and alert, in full control of both body and mind.

One . . . Two . . . Three . . . More and more awake and alert . . .

Four . . . Five . . . Six . . . More awake, feeling great . . .

Seven . . . Eight . . . Nearly awake now.

Nine . . . Ten . . . Open your eyes; you are awake and alert.

Take your time . . . stretch . . . and come all the way back.

Meditation 2: Healing Meditation with Dolphins

With your eyes gently closed, take a few deep breaths. Imagine that you can breathe out the tensions and stresses in your body. . . . Imagine that you can breathe in the beautiful energy all around you. . . .

Let each breath take you deeper and deeper into a beautiful state of relaxation.

[Pause for fifteen seconds to allow the breath to relax the body.]

Now relax all your muscles. Relax the muscles of your face and jaw. Let go of all tightness and all tension in these muscles. . . .

Relax the muscles of your neck and your shoulders. . . .

Relax your arms. . . . Completely relax the muscles of your back, both the upper back and the lower back. . . . Let go of all tightness and all tension in these muscles. . . .

Relax the muscles of your stomach and abdomen, so that your breathing stays perfectly relaxed. . . .

Relax completely the muscles of your legs, so that now your entire body is in a state of deep peace. . . .

Let any outside noises or distractions only deepen your level even more.

Imagine or visualize or feel a beautiful light above your head. You can choose the color or colors. This light will deepen your level and heal your body. . . .

Let the light flow into your body through the top of your head. It illuminates the brain and spinal cord, healing these tissues and deepening your level even more. . . .

Let the light flow down, from above to below, like a beautiful wave of light, touching every cell, every fiber, and every organ in your body with peace and love and healing. . . .

Wherever your body needs healing, let the light be very strong and powerful in this area. . . . [Fifteen-second pause.]

And let the rest of the light flow all the way to your feet, so that your body is filled with this beautiful light. . . .

Now, imagine or feel the light completely surrounding the outside of your body as well, as if you were wrapped in a beautiful bubble or cocoon of light. This protects you, heals your skin, and deepens your level even more. . . .

Counting backwards from ten to one, let each number back take you deeper into the relaxed state.

Ten . . . Nine . . . Eight . . . Deeper and deeper with each number back . . .

Seven . . . Six . . . Five . . . More and more peaceful and relaxed . . .

Four . . . Three . . . So calm and serene . . .

Two . . . Nearly there . . .

One . . . Good.

In this wonderful state of peace and tranquillity, imagine yourself walking down a beautiful staircase . . . down, down . . . deeper and deeper . . . down, down . . . each step down deepening your level even more. . . .

As you reach the bottom of the steps, in front of you is a beautiful garden . . . a garden of peace and beauty and safety . . . a sanctuary. . . .

Walk into this garden and find a place to rest. . . .

Your body, still filled by the light and surrounded by the light, continues to heal and to recuperate. The deepest levels of your mind can open up. You can remember everything. You can experience all levels of your multidimensional self. You are far greater than your body or your brain.

If you are ever uncomfortable with any memory or any feeling or any experience during this meditation, just float above it and watch from a distance, as if you were watching a movie. If you are still uncomfortable, float back to the garden and rest there, or even open your eyes and return to full, waking consciousness.

If you are not uncomfortable, stay with the images and the feelings. You are always in control.

Float above your body in the garden . . . and travel to a beautiful and ancient island, surrounded by blue and turquoise waters. . . . This is an island of healing. . . .

You can walk on the beautiful beach . . . feel the warmth of the sun . . . feel the gentle breeze.

Embedded in the floor of the sea, a short distance out from the beach, are some large and powerful crystals . . . these are healing crystals.

The crystals impart a healing energy to the water.

Wade into the water, as much or as little as you want. . . . You can feel the tingling, healing energy in the water. . . .

The energy transmitted from the crystals to the water is absorbed by your skin and body. . . . [Fifteen-second pause.]

Now imagine that some very tame and very loving dolphins come to be with you in the water. . . .

Dolphins are master healers. They know just where in your body the healing needs to occur. . . . They point to these areas. . . .

They help the water to heal. [Thirty-second pause.]

You can swim and play with them if you wish. . . .

Now it is time to leave the water, so you say good-bye for now . . . but you can always return . . . whenever you need or wish. . . .

As you leave the water, you notice you are immediately dry. . . . This is such a special water. . . .

As you sit on the beach, reflect upon the areas of your body that are healing. . . .

Use your imagination and become the old illness. . . .

How do you affect this person whose body you are in? . . .

What messages have you been trying to convey? . . .

What role do you play in his or her life? . . .

Are you useful in some manner? . . .

How can you be healed? . . .

Now switch roles and become yourself again. . . . Imagine your life without the illness. . . .

What have you learned about your illness? . . .

How have you compensated for the lack of illness? . . .

Visualize and feel the illness gone and your body whole again . . . healed . . . filled with light. . . . [Thirty-second pause.]

Floating above the beach, you return to the beautiful garden.

Your body in the garden has been filled with the beautiful light. It has been healing and refreshing.

Now it is time to return to full waking consciousness.

Counting upwards from one to ten, let each number awaken you more and more. By the count of ten you can open your eyes and you will be wide awake and alert, in full control of both body and mind.

One . . . Two . . . Three . . . More and more awake and alert . . .

Four . . . Five . . . Six . . . More awake, feeling great . . .

Seven . . . Eight . . . Nearly awake now.

Nine . . . Ten . . . Open your eyes; you are awake and alert.

Take your time . . . stretch . . . and come all the way back.

About the Author

Dr. Weiss maintains a private practice in Miami, Florida, where his offices include well-trained and highly experienced psychologists and social workers who also use regression therapy and the techniques of spiritual psychotherapy in their work. In addition, Dr. Weiss conducts seminars and experiential workshops nationally and internationally as well as training programs for professionals. He has recorded a series of audiotapes and CDs in which he helps you discover and learn techniques of meditation, healing, deep relaxation, regression, and other visualization exercises.

For more information, please contact:

The Weiss Institute
6701 Sunset Drive, Suite 201
Miami, Florida 33143
Phone: (305) 661-6610
Fax: (305) 661-5311
e-mail: in2healing@aol.com
website: www.brianweiss.com